T0305757

Beyond the Dollar and the Euro

Reshaping the
International Monetary System
through Regional Monetary
Cooperation in East Asia

Beyond the Dollar and the Euro

Reshaping the International Monetary System through Regional Monetary Cooperation in East Asia

Yung Chul PARK
Korea University, Korea

Il Houng LEE
Korea Institute for International Economic Policy, Korea

 World Scientific

NEW JERSEY · LONDON · SINGAPORE · BEIJING · SHANGHAI · HONG KONG · TAIPEI · CHENNAI · TOKYO

Published by

World Scientific Publishing Co. Pte. Ltd.

5 Toh Tuck Link, Singapore 596224

USA office: 27 Warren Street, Suite 401-402, Hackensack, NJ 07601

UK office: 57 Shelton Street, Covent Garden, London WC2H 9HE

Library of Congress Cataloging-in-Publication Data
Names: Pak, Yŏng-ch'ŏl, 1939–   author. | Lee, Il Houng, author.
Title: Beyond the dollar and the euro : reshaping the international monetary
    system through regional monetary cooperation in East Asia / Yung Chul Park
    (Korea University, Korea), Il Houng Lee (Korea Institute for International
    Economic Policy, Korea).
Description: New Jersey : World Scientific, 2016. | Includes bibliographical
    references and index.
Identifiers: LCCN 2015047735 | ISBN 9789814749435 (hardcover : alk. paper)
Subjects: LCSH: Monetary policy--East Asia--International cooperation. |
    International finance--East Asia. | East Asia--Foreign economic relations. |
    Global Financial Crisis, 2008–2009.
Classification: LCC HG1270.5 .P353 2016 | DDC 332.4/5095--dc23
LC record available at http://lccn.loc.gov/2015047735

British Library Cataloguing-in-Publication Data
A catalogue record for this book is available from the British Library.

Copyright © 2016 by Korea Institute for International Economic Policy

All rights reserved.

Desk Editor: Qi Xiao

Typeset by Stallion Press
Email: enquiries@stallionpress.com

Printed in Singapore

Acknowledgments

This book has its origins in a research project initiated by the Korea Institute for International Economic Policy (KIEP), Korea's leading think tank. The research was initiated on December 1, 2013 and finalized on December 30, 2015, with the goal of analyzing changes in the world economy since the global financial crisis from a variety of economic, functional, and analytical perspectives. The authors would like to thank KIEP for its financial support, which was essential to completion of the project.

The Korea Institute for International Economic Policy (KIEP) was founded in 1989 as a government-funded independent economic research institute. KIEP advises the government on all major international economic policy issues and carries out research on various aspects of world economy, such as international finance, macroeconomics, trade and investment, and regional studies.

Contents

Acknowledgments   v
About the Authors   xi

Chapter 1 Introduction   **1**
            Yung Chul Park

**Chapter 2 Use of National Currencies for Trade Settlement
            in East Asia: A Proposal**   **9**
            Il Houng Lee and Yung Chul Park

    1. Introduction   9
    2. Trade Patterns and Financial Openness:
       Preconditions of ASEAN-5, China, Japan,
       and Korea   12
       2.1. Trade Openness   12
       2.2. Proliferation of Free Trade Agreements   13
       2.3. Intra-regional Trade   14
       2.4. Intra-industry Trade   17
       2.5. Financial Openness   20
    3. Progress in the Internationalization of the
       Renminbi   21
       3.1. Renminbi as a Currency of Settlement   22
       3.2. Renminbi Settlement Services and Interbank
           Market   24
       3.3. Interbank Market for the Renminbi   25
       3.4. Renminbi as a Reserve Currency   26
       3.5. The Shanghai Pilot Free Trade Zone   28
       3.6. Policies to Promote Investments
           in RMB-denominated Financial Assets   28

4. Objectives and the Potential Size of the Currency
   Scheme in East Asia 30
   4.1. Objectives 30
   4.2. Potential Size 33
5. Structure of the System 36
   5.1. Convertibility 36
   5.2. Clearing and Settlement 37
   5.3. Interbank Foreign Exchange Markets 38
   5.4. Investment Vehicles 38
   5.5. Adjustments of Imbalances of Holdings
        of National Currencies 39
6. Benefits and Risks 40
   6.1. Benefits 40
   6.2. Relative Advantages 41
   6.3. Risks and Their Management 44
7. Concluding Remarks 44
References 46
Appendix 48

**Chapter 3 Issues and Prospects of International Monetary
          Reforms: East Asian Perspectives 49**
Yung Chul Park

1. Introduction 49
2. Reserve Currency System 52
   2.1. The Demise of the US Dollar? 52
   2.2. Special Drawing Rights (SDR) 53
   2.3. A Multiple Reserve Currency System? 54
3. The Euro, the RMB, and Currencies of Other
   Emerging Economies 55
   3.1. The Euro 55
   3.2. RMB 56
   3.3. Other Currencies of Emerging Economies 59
4. Capital Controls and Exchange Rate Regimes 60
   4.1. IMF Advocacy of Capital Controls 60
   4.2. Effectiveness, Instruments, and Scope
        of Capital Inflow Controls 62

5. ASEAN+3 and Regional Liquidity Support
   Arrangements   63
   5.1. Evolution of the Mutual Liquidity Support
        System in East Asia   63
   5.2. Issues in Regional Arrangements in East Asia   64
   5.3. CMIM's Viability   65
6. Swaps as a Global Safety Net   67
   6.1. Swaps among Major Central Banks   68
   6.2. A Cooperative Arrangement among Major
        Central Banks   71
   7. Conclusion   72
   References   73

**Chapter 4 The Euro-Area Sovereign Debt and Banking
            Crises: Perspectives from East Asia   77**
            Yung Chul Park

1. Introduction and Overview   77
2. Causes, Triggers, and Consequences
   of the Capital Account Crises   82
   2.1. Causes and Triggers: East Asia   83
   2.2. Causes and Triggers: Euro Area   85
   2.3. Flaws in the EEMU Architecture   89
   2.4. Recovery and Relative Efficiency of
        Resolution Programs in Asia and Europe   92
3. Program Design and Implementation:
   Asian Crisis Lessons   95
   3.1. Resolution Strategy: Growth First or
        Austerity First?   96
   3.2. Failure of Prompt Response   99
   3.3. Structural Reforms   102
   3.4. Austerity and the Failure of Expenditure
        Switching   107
4. Collaboration with EU: Independence
   and Credibility of the IMF   109
   4.1. The Role of the IMF in the Troika's Crisis
        Management   110

5. Summary and Conclusion   114
References   118
Appendix   122

**Chapter 5   Shaping the Future of the IMS: Regionalization
               of Selected Asian Currencies   131**
Il Houng Lee

1. Introduction: A Need to Create an Asian
   Monetary System   131
2. Demand for a Reserve Currency   135
   2.1. RMB as a Candidate for Reserve Currency   135
   2.2. A Long-term Process   136
3. Possible Shape of the New IMS   139
   3.1. Time for a Change to the IMS   139
   3.2. Possible Framework of a New IMS   141
4. Incentives and Risks for Member Countries   148
   4.1. Incentives   149
   4.2. Risks   151
   4.3. Other Economic Considerations   154
   4.4. Geopolitical Challenges   155
5. Conclusion   156
References   157

Chapter 6   Conclusion   159
Yung Chul Park and Il Houng Lee

Index   161

About the Authors

Yung Chul Park is a distinguished professor in the division of international studies, Korea University. He previously served as the chief economic adviser to the President of Korea, as president of the Korea Development Institute, and as president of the Korea Institute of Finance. He also worked for the International Monetary Fund. He has written and edited several books, including *Monetary and Financial Cooperation in East Asia: The Relevance of European Experience* (Oxford University Press, 2010).

Il Houng Lee is the president of KIEP. He is also a visiting professor at Jilin University in China. He served as the Ambassador for International Cooperation and G20 Sherpa of Republic of Korea in 2013–2015. Prior to his appointment as the Ambassador, he was with the IMF for more than 20 years. He earned his B.A. in Economics at LSE and a Ph.D. in Economics at Warwick University in the UK. His latest contribution is the chapter "Tri-polar Cluster System: A Proposal" (pp. 193–198) in the book *Bretton Woods: The Next 70 Years* (Reinventing Bretton Woods Committee, 2015).

Chapter 1

Introduction

Yung Chul Park

This book is a collection of four essays, all of which address some of the issues pertaining to the reform of the international monetary system (IMS). There is a general consensus among economists and policymakers from both advanced and emerging economies that deficiency and instability of the IMS are the root causes of periodic regional and global financial crises and a high degree of volatility of global financial markets. The weaknesses of the IMS were also responsible for the severity, contagion, and persistency of the 2008 financial crisis.

In response to the growing need for redressing the failures of the IMS, the French G20 summit in 2011 identified a number of areas where the reform of the IMS was called for and its leaders agreed to cooperate to move forward with the required system overhaul.

However, since then the G20 and other international fora have been preoccupied with other more pressing global economic issues such as global recession with deflation and the euro-area crisis, the reform of the IMS was set aside as of secondary importance. This by no means suggests that urgency of the reform has subsided. By all accounts, the need for reform has remained critical ever since. Countries in every continent have been nervously waiting for when and to what extent the US Fed is going to raise its policy rate. One might ask why the expected tightening of monetary policy in the United States provokes such financial market volatility and poses such uncertainty and danger of setting off financial crisis in many emerging countries, including those with a flexible exchange rate system.

According to Rey (2013), the answer to this question is rather simple. In a financially integrated global economy, financial linkages among countries generate a global financial cycle set by the financing conditions in the main global centers of international finance — the US being the dominant center — that govern the conditions in the rest of the world regardless of the exchange rate regime (Rey 2013).[1] At the same time, the euro-area crisis has somewhat diminished the global reach of the euro as a major international currency. China's currency, the RMB, will likely emerge as a major international currency. However, recent developments have lowered the growth prospect and have cast doubts on its ascendance as a major international currency. Despite these developments, there has been no serious discussion of the reform of the IMS and the supremacy of the US dollar remains unchallenged.

China's growth will inevitably slow down, but it will sustain its international role as the second largest economy. In the new milieu of free trade fervor, by virtue of its large size and a commanding share in intraregional trade, China has been at the center of trade integration in East Asia. While negotiating FTAs with regional partners, China has also been active in elevating the status of its currency — the RMB — to a global as well as a regional unit of account and medium of exchange. Over a relatively short period since it initiated the pilot program for the RMB internationalization in 2009, China has made great strides in expanding the use of its currency for trade settlements throughout East Asia.

Soon after the start of the pilot program, China took steps to broaden its scope of the initial program by removing some of the restrictions on capital account transactions and foreign investments in domestic financial assets to support RMB's internationalization. However, China was not prepared to embark on a sweeping financial reform, which was required for currency internationalization. Instead, the country chose to promote first the use of the RMB for settling trade with its neighboring economies rather than internationalizing it.[2]

---

[1] In the finance literature explaining the global stock market integration, a number of authors search for world factors common to all stock markets that drive the co-movement in stock prices and the presence of a strong group factor, a world factor constructed from country indices by principal components, value-weighting, or some other method of aggregating the indexes (see Blackburn and Chidambaran, 2011).

[2] Internationalization of a currency is defined as a currency's use outside the issuer's borders, including purchases of goods, services, and financial assets in transactions by

If Chinese strategy is viable and promising, then some other members of ASEAN+3 (the members of the Association of Southeast Asian Nations plus China, Japan, and Korea), who are not ready to open their financial markets and relinquish control over the capital account, may find that the path China has taken presents a new — and perhaps more tenable, — approach, allowing the use of their currencies outside their countries for trade settlement.

Despite a few landmark achievements such as the Chiang Mai Initiative (CMI), financial deepening and monetary integration in East Asia has been slow. Meanwhile, proliferation of FTAs in East Asia and China's successful accession to the WTO have enabled faster progress in trade integration among the regional economies. Building on the expanding intra-regional trade, the authors of Chapter 2 propose the creation of a multilateral currency arrangement where some of the national currencies could be used for trade settlement within the cooperative framework of ASEAN+3. This would facilitate closer financial integration and greater flexibility of the Asian currencies against the US dollar without being kept captive by the slow progress in capital account liberalization in some countries.

Although any member with a relatively open trade and financial regime is a potential participant, at the initial stage of development, China, Japan, Korea, and possibly some of ASEAN-5 countries appear to be the most appropriate candidates to construct — and benefit from — the scheme as they have established an institutional base broad enough to accommodate such a regional cooperative arrangement.

Chapter 3 advances the debates on reforming the international monetary system by analyzing its key aspects. These are: reserve currencies, including alternatives to the US dollar; the future of the euro and Chinese RMB; the role of capital controls; regional monetary arrangements, particularly the Chiang Mai Initiative and its successors; and the use of swap agreements among central banks.

The author concludes that the dollar will remain the dominant reserve currency. At this stage of development, no other countries could replace

---

nonresidents. It is essentially an organic, evolutionary, and market-driven process (see Kenen, 2011).

the dollar simply because they do not have the capacity to issue large quantities of safe assets such as US Treasury bills to meet the global needs of liquidity. The Special Drawing Right (SDR), created by the IMF in 1969, is not a money, but a right for a central bank to obtain dollars, euros, or other currencies of wide international use. Special Drawing Rights could serve as a reserve currency and asset, but politically it is almost impossible to increase its supply enough to replace or complement the dollar. This is because as a potential claim on some currencies, SDR must be underwritten by the central banks that issue these currencies. New SDRs are effectively new dollars, euros, yen, and other widely traded currencies. But no one knows which currencies will be used — and when. No central bank will ever want to create large amounts of money over which it has no control.

There are two other potential major currencies in addition to the dollar — the euro and the Chinese RMB. The author argues that the euro will survive the ongoing euro zone crisis and that the outlook for internationalization of the RMB, which depends largely on the prospects of China's financial liberalization and rapid growth, is not entirely promising. However, this has not dissuaded a number of observers including the World Bank (2011) from arguing that the US dollar will eventually be replaced by a multi-currency system made up of the dollar, the euro, the RMB, and currencies of other emerging economies. Is a multi-reserve currency system viable? Economists are divided on this question as it is difficult to weigh the relative importance of merits and demerits of the system.

On management of capital flows in a new global financial environment, the IMF position had long oscillated between firm hostility and reluctant acceptance before changing its position to accept capital controls as a means of moderating volatility of capital flows (IMF, 2012). Refining the instruments, and making them better attuned to present-day markets, may bring further changes to the conventional wisdom.

As for the prospect of regional liquidity support arrangement known as the Chiang Mai Initiative Multilateralization (CMIM), the 2008 financial crisis and euro-area sovereign debt crisis have dimmed much of the earlier hope that it would become operational. The European debt crisis has made it clear that deep regional monetary integration is more difficult than was officially recognized.

However, Kawai and Park (2015) believe that CMIM can be re-designed as an integrated crisis prevention (provision of temporary foreign exchange liquidity support) and crisis response (for cases of currency crises requiring strong macroeconomic adjustment policies) mechanism. If a country faces temporary foreign exchange liquidity shortage, such as an unexpected episode of rapid short-term capital outflows, and the country passes the CMIM pre-qualification criteria, then CMIM should provide the liquidity to the country without any IMF link or conditionality up to the full amount of the country's swap quota. Even then, it would still only be applicable to smaller countries.

Finally, Chapter 3 finishes with reviewing the prospect of the spread of swap agreements among central banks. In the aftermath of the 2008 collapse of Lehman Brothers, swaps have been activated on a larger scale than before. It explores whether the use of swaps portends a new form of international monetary cooperation.

Chapter 4 discusses some of the implications of the euro-area crisis for the reform of the IMS. The European Union (EU) has been a major trading partner to ASEAN+3. By 2007, the EU had emerged as the largest export market for ASEAN+3, overtaking the United States by absorbing more than 16 percent of East Asia's total merchandise exports. Reflecting the ongoing recession and euro-area crisis, it has fallen behind the United States since 2011.

By the middle of 2009, the 2008 global financial crisis turned market sentiment against the prospect of those euro-area economies running large fiscal and current account deficits, particularly Greece, Ireland, and Portugal, shutting them out of external funding markets. This change in market sentiment claimed Greece as the first casualty of a capital account crisis that has spread to Ireland and Portugal, rocking the entire euro area for more than five years.

Through June 2015 the EU and the IMF have provided €403 billion in financial support. Of this, €240 billion, or more than 42 percent, has been for bailing out Greece. The IMF contribution to all three countries amounts to €106.5 billion, equal to 56 percent of its total lending.

Despite this huge financial support and imposition of fiscal austerity, financial restructuring, and supply side reform, the first two Greek bailout programs ended in failure and the EU and Greece have agreed to a third program. The prospect of Portugal hangs in the balance and only Ireland has been successful in returning to robust growth.

While economic mismanagement should be blamed for creating a fertile ground for speculation in Greece, Ireland, and Portugal, it is also true that structural flaws in the euro architecture played a significant part in the buildup and propagation of the crisis. One of the most serious structural flaws of EMU has been the absence of a mechanism for adjusting balance of payment imbalances among the members.

The Stability and Growth Pact (SGP) and no bailout clause — the two keystones for intra-regional stability in the euro area — are designed to prevent the emergence of large fiscal and external imbalances among members. The SGP has been repeatedly breached, and the no bailout clause lost its credibility long ago. As long as the current account deficit could be financed with foreign loans, governments were inclined to set aside or defer addressing the underlying problems. For this reason, the countries in the southern periphery were prone to running large current account deficits. When deficits are persistent and large, market's remedy can be brutal: it abruptly stops lending.[3] Since the crisis, the SGP has been replaced by more stringent rules, but whether there is any realistic chance of establishing a fiscal union[4] remains uncertain. The euro-area crisis conforms to what has been accepted for a long time that monetary union without political union is not a viable arrangement.

The global economy suffers from a similar adjustment problem that has besieged the euro area. For the sake of argument and following Rey (2013), suppose there is a global financial cycle set by the financing conditions in the main global centers of international finance, such as the center in the United States, that govern the conditions in the rest of

---

[3] For a more extensive discussion see Wyplosz (2014).
[4] See Mody (2015) and Wolf (2014) who argues that "the EU must avoid another useless fight over its fiscal rules and instead use political capital to foster growth".

the world regardless of the exchange rate regime. Under these conditions, the global economy will not be able to establish any reliable mechanism for adjusting balance of payments imbalances between countries regardless of the exchange rate regime they adopt.

In light of all this, Chapter 5 further develops the idea proposed in Chapter 2 for a currency arrangement among Asian economies, e.g., ASEAN+3, involving an agreement to settle their current account transactions in any of the few selected local currencies. The intended outcome of this proposal is a tri-polar system that will be able to address some of the challenges noted earlier. The dominance of the US dollar as the main world reserve currency will continue for the foreseeable future. Yet various events, including the financial crisis, point to the need for an alternative system that will strengthen market discipline rather than having to rely excessively on policy coordination. The rise of Asian economies led by China provides a unique opportunity for regionalization of selected Asian currencies, namely settling current account transactions among Asian economies using selected local currencies.

It is up to the market to determine which currency it will use, but one should not forget that it is the government that provides the market framework when a market is created. In this regard, if governments in ASEAN+3 can agree to create a framework in the best interest of all parties concerned, the market will decide whether to use it or not. International agreement for a change in the IMS has proven to be almost impossible, but the euro, despite all its drawbacks as discussed above, has shown that progress is possible at the regional level. Nevertheless, one needs to be careful, that such an agreement does not create a framework that goes ahead of political commitments nor impose rules that become internally inconsistent.

To begin, relevant governments could start putting in place similar measures taken by China for RMB internationalization. Then, it will depend on the market to determine how fast it wants to shape an alternative international monetary system. Most likely, a two-tier and a tri-polar system will emerge. The first tier will consist of currencies mainly used for medium of exchange and unit of account while the second tier will be for the use of currencies as store of value. Once the necessary legal framework is in place, the US dollar, euro, and the RMB will likely dominate, forming a tri-polar system along each of which various local currencies will be used specific to the locality. For the second tier, i.e., as the store of value, the US dollar will retain its hegemony for a few more decades. Gradually, these two tiers will merge, forming a new monetary order.

Chapter 2

Use of National Currencies for Trade Settlement in East Asia: A Proposal

Il Houng Lee and Yung Chul Park

1. Introduction

Achieving deeper financial and monetary integration in East Asia has been an elusive goal. In the aftermath of the 1997–8 Asian financial crisis, ASEAN+3 (the members of the Association of Southeast Asian Nations plus China, Japan, and Korea) realized the urgency of constructing regional cooperative arrangements for regional economic integration and expanding the scope of policy coordination to prevent future crises and help safeguard the region from financial spillovers from outside the region. In 2000 they decided to create a regional liquidity support system known as the Chiang Mai Initiative, which was later restructured and renamed the Chiang Mai Initiative Multilateralization (CMIM).

Since then, other regional initiatives followed to expand and complement the role of the CMIM.[1] As memories of the 1997–8 financial crisis faded and financial stability returned, ASEAN+3 momentum for regional cooperation grew until the region experienced the contagion from the 2008 global financial crisis. After years of negotiating to reorganize and increase the size of CMIM finances, CMIM was expected to act. Markets

---

[1] The Economic Review and Policy Dialogue is a non-binding surveillance process structured as a peer review, which is supported by the ASEAN+3 Macroeconomic Research Office located in Singapore and established in 2011. The Asian Bond Market Development Initiative sets the stage for creating regional bond markets and integrating the ASEAN+3 financial market.

were watching closely to see what role CMIM could play in insulating the region from the onslaught of vagaries of global financial market.

Some of the member countries suffered severe shortages of US dollar liquidity, which drove them to the edge of another financial meltdown. Yet, despite their acute need, none of the countries would consider drawing down liquidity from the CMIM. Accordingly, both global and regional financial markets have ignored the existence of this system.[2] This ineffectiveness of the CMIM, together with travails of the euro zone as a monetary union in recent years, has dampened further interest of the member states of ASEAN+3 in consolidating regional monetary and financial cooperation.

While regional efforts at financial cooperation and integration have languished, ASEAN+3 members have been actively pursuing trade liberalization by initiating and concluding negotiations for a number of bilateral and plurilateral free trade agreements (FTAs), both within and outside the region. The proliferation of FTAs has been a new driver for regional economic integration.

In this new milieu of free trade fervor, by virtue of its large size and a commanding share in intra-regional trade, China has been at the center of trade integration in East Asia. While negotiating FTAs with regional partners, China has also been active in elevating the status of its currency — the renminbi — to a global as well as regional unit of account and medium of exchange. Over a relatively short period since it initiated the pilot program for renminbi internationalization in 2009, China has made great strides in expanding the use of its currency for trade settlements throughout East Asia.

Theory and historical experiences of other countries suggest that countries wishing to internationalize their currencies need to satisfy first a set of preconditions including financial reform that liberalize financial markets, deregulate capital account transactions, and make their currencies convertible. China was far from meeting these conditions.

---

[2] Because of the limitations of the CMIM as a regional liquidity support system and their aversion to approaching the IMF for its short-run lending facilities, many ASEAN+3 members have chosen to accumulate more foreign exchange reserves than before and sought to secure liquidity through bilateral currency swap arrangements with countries within and outside the region.

Realizing that it was not prepared to embark on a sweeping financial reform, China chose first to promote the use of the renminbi for settling trade with its neighboring economies.

Soon after the start of the pilot program, China broadened the scope of the initial program by removing some of the restrictions on capital account transactions and foreign investments in domestic financial assets to support renminbi's growing international use.[3] Yet, growth of demand for renminbi has stabilized recently, indicating perhaps the difficulty achieving currency internationalization with limited capital account convertibility. It is possible to move the agenda forward if some other members of ASEAN+3 are willing to take the path that China has taken without opening their financial markets.

The purpose of this chapter is to develop such a currency scheme among the ASEAN-5 member states and China, Japan, and Korea. Any country with a relatively open trade and financial regime is a potential participant, but these countries are the most appropriate candidates. Each has established an institutional base that is broad enough to accommodate such a regional cooperative arrangement.

This chapter proposes a multilateral currency system for trade settlement within the cooperative framework of ASEAN+3. The first section examines regional patterns and structure of trade to gauge the scope of cooperation and the potential benefits from the use of national currencies in trade settlements.[4] Are the trade and financial environment conducive to the construction and operations of such a system?

The second section turns to China's experience with permitting greater use of the renminbi both regionally and globally. Since China is the largest trading partner to all other members of ASEAN+3 as the center country in East Asia's trade network, and has been at the forefront of currency internationalization, China's approach could be emulated by others in the region.

---

[3] Internationalization of currency is defined as a currency's use outside the issuer's borders, including for purchases of goods, services, and financial assets in transactions by nonresidents. It is essentially an organic, evolutionary, and market-driven process. See Kenen (2011).

[4] In this chapter, the geographical coverage of East Asia includes the 13 countries of ASEAN+3.

The third section discusses the objectives and the potential size of the currency scheme while the proposed structure of scheme is outlined in the fourth section. Since some of the potential members are likely to run deficits with other members and outflows of currencies of deficit would occur at the initial phase of development, it would be helpful to contain the volatility of capital flows to get the currency scheme off the drawing board. The fifth section examines benefits and risks of the currency scheme, followed by concluding remarks.

2. Trade Patterns and Financial Openness: Preconditions of ASEAN-5, China, Japan, and Korea

China, Japan, and Korea and some of the ASEAN-5 countries will consider participating in the new currency scheme only if they could see the possibility of reaping the benefits of a wider use of their currencies for current account settlement. The benefit will largely arise from lower exchange rate risks and conversion costs, and at the macroeconomic level, from the need to hold a smaller amount of international reserves. Later as these currencies become convertible, the benefit will include reduced cost of financing and investment within the region. Thus, the viability of the new system would, among other things, depend on:

— the degree of openness of trade and the future prospects for trade liberalization
— the share of intra-regional trade and the structure of intra-industry trade
— the degree of financial openness and the future prospect for financial market opening and capital account liberalization.

2.1. Trade Openness

The amount of the benefit would, other things being equal, be positively related to the degree of openness of the trade regime. Historically, the degree has been high in East Asia. From the early 1990s to 2007, all of the

Table 1.   Openness of the Trade Regime: Ratio of Total Trade to GDP

(Unit: %)

	2003–07	2008–12	2013–14
China	60.2	49.1	42.7
Japan	24.2	26.6	32.0
Korea	64.9	90.6	80.1
ASEAN-10	125.2	104.3	102.9

Sources: IMF DOT, World Bank.

ASEAN+3 countries except Indonesia saw a sharp increase in their total trade relative to GDP. The economic slowdown in the aftermath of the 2008 global financial crisis and the subsequent euro zone debt crisis has caused further contraction of trade in China, Korea, and ASEAN-5. In the case of Japan, openness index rose during the last two years due to the large depreciation of the yen. As shown in Table 1, notwithstanding the setback, except Japan, all other countries in the group still heavily depend on exports relative to emerging economies in other regions.

2.2. Proliferation of Free Trade Agreements

There has been a large increase in the number of FTAs in East Asia. At the end of April 2015, there were 84 FTAs and more under negotiation in Asia, ASEAN+3, India, Hong Kong SAR (Special Administrative Region), and Taiwan (province of China). The member states of ASEAN+3 have concluded a number of FTAs with partners within and outside the regional grouping. Among larger plurilateral ones are the ASEAN FTA and the three ASEAN+1 FTAs with China, Japan, and Korea. They have also initiated negotiations for other bilateral and multilateral FTAs. China and Korea have concluded a bilateral FTA recently. ASEAN+3 are participating in the negotiation for a 16-country FTA that includes Australia, India, and New Zealand through the mechanism of the Regional Comprehensive Economic Partnership.

Although it is beyond the scope of this chapter to analyze the causal relation between the increase in the number of FTAs and use of national currencies for trade settlement, recent studies by Kawai and Wignaraja (2013) and Wignaraja (2013) suggest that the proliferation could have positive effects on the construction of the currency scheme. In their examination of the results of a number of independent country surveys as well as the Asian Development Bank and Asian Development Bank Institute firm-level survey in 2007–08, they show that the increase in the number of FTAs in Asia contributed to expanding trade among firms, and prevented collapse of intra- and inter-regional trade during the 2008 global financial crisis.

More important to our study is the finding of these surveys that FTA use by enterprises in East Asia has been higher than expected, and it is increasing as more firms plan to utilize them. If this is the response at the firm level, one may then surmise that the widespread use of FTAs therefore points to the possibility that firms in East Asia — large and small — may also actively participate in the regional currency scheme for trade settlement to the extent that they are fully informed of its benefits.

The increase in the number of FTAs will strengthen the case for the use of national currencies for trade settlement, and more so if the existing bilateral and plurilateral FTAs are integrated into a large region-wide FTA, e.g., the FTA of Asia Pacific (FTAAP). The increase in the number of countries joining the currency scheme could facilitate negotiations for forming such a region wide FTA, and resuscitate construction of the FTA among China, Japan, and Korea — a parallel negotiation that has been making slow progress for more than a decade since 2003 when the three countries agreed to a feasibility study.

2.3. Intra-regional Trade

a. ASEAN+3

The greater the potential gains from developing the currency scheme, the larger the intra-regional share in ASEAN+3's total trade. As shown in Figure 1, intra-regional trade in East Asia suffered a severe setback during the 1997–8 Asian financial crisis. The share returned to the pre-crisis level around 2003 and since then has remained broadly at around 40 percent.

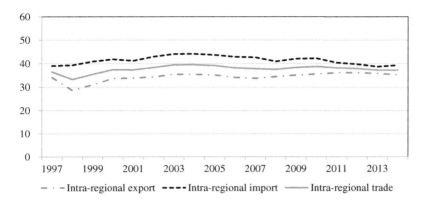

Figure 1.   Intra-regional Trade Share in ASEAN+3

(Unit: % of Total)

Sources: IMF DOT.

China provides the largest market for exports and the second largest for imports to all other economies in East Asia. Compared to the Economic and Monetary Union in 1989 — 10 years before the creation of the euro — the proportion of intra-regional trade is much lower in East Asia, but its growth has been impressive, given the rapid increase in total trade during the relatively short history of economic integration in the region.[5]

b. Trade with China

With the rise of China as a global trader and the major assembler of parts, components, and other intermediate inputs, two-way trade of other East Asian countries with China has been growing and is expected to rise. Among the members of ASEAN+3, the increase in the dependence of ASEAN-5 on China for their exports has been remarkable (see Figure 2). In 2000, they shipped less than 4 percent of their exports to China; one and a half decades later this has grown to more than 15 percent largely at the expense of their exports to the United States. Japan and Korea also depend heavily on China's market as they send on average more than

---

[5] In 1989, the average ratio of intra-regional trade in the euro area was 69 percent for imports and 66 percent for exports.

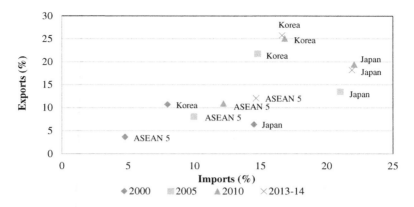

Figure 2.   Share of Trade with China by Country or Group

(**Unit: %**)

Sources: UN COMTRADE Database.

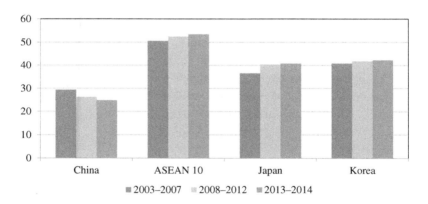

Figure 3.   Share of Trade with ASEAN+3 by Country or Group

(**Unit: %**)

Sources: IMF DOT.

22 percent of their exports to the country. Regarding intra-regional trade, China trades relatively more with the countries outside than those within East Asia.

China's regional trade share was smallest at about 26 percent compared to ASEAN (54 percent), Korea (43 percent), and Japan (40 percent) during 2013–14 (see Figure 3). ASEAN's imports from China, in particular, have continued to rise significantly in recent years. While China trades

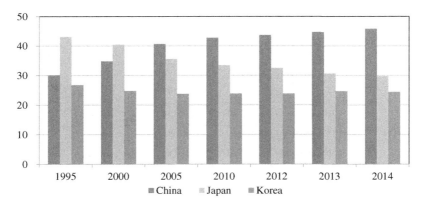

Figure 4.   Share in Intra-regional Trade among China, Japan, and Korea

(Unit: %)

Sources: IMF DOT.

relatively more with non-ASEAN+3 countries, given the huge absolute magnitude of its trade, its share in intra-trade among China, Japan, and Korea is highest at close to 50 percent in 2014 from about 30 percent in 1995, mostly at the expense of Japan (see Figure 4).

2.4. Intra-industry Trade

a. ASEAN

The network trade centering on China has long been a defining feature of East Asia's intra-industry trade structure. The available data confirm that there has been little change in this structure.[6] Table 2 presents five-year averages of the Grubel and Lloyd (1975) index of the three categories of intra-industry trade — parts and components, capital goods, and consumer goods — of ASEAN-5 vis-à-vis China as the center country for the two sub-periods from 2000 to 2009, and a similar average for the 2010–14 (post-global financial crisis) periods.

As expected, except Indonesia during the 2005–09 period, parts and components display the highest indices. In fact, the value of this index did not change to any noticeable degree throughout the observation

---

[6] This is also true for ASEAN+3. See Table 7 in appendix.

Table 2.   Intra-industry Trade of ASEAN-5 with China: Grubel and Lloyd Index

	Category	2000–04 Average	2005–09 Average	2010–14 Average
Thailand	Parts and components	0.91	0.75	0.95
	Capital goods	0.47	0.91	0.57
	Consumer goods	0.80	0.74	0.82
Indonesia	Parts and components	0.58	0.27	0.86
	Capital goods	0.31	0.27	0.06
	Consumer goods	0.38	0.40	0.48
Philippines	Parts and components	0.64	0.67	0.89
	Capital goods	0.63	0.68	0.72
	Consumer goods	0.46	0.24	0.31
Malaysia	Parts and components	0.88	0.76	0.84
	Capital goods	0.58	0.62	0.63
	Consumer goods	0.27	0.36	0.31
Singapore	Parts and components	0.95	0.83	0.77
	Capital goods	0.71	0.51	0.50
	Consumer goods	0.42	0.71	0.81

Sources: UN COMTRADE Database.

period. A similar pattern, albeit at a relatively lower level and again except for Indonesia, is noted for capital goods. The indices for consumer goods are lower, except for Thailand and Singapore, especially in recent years.

b. China, Japan, and Korea

The indices for parts and components and capital goods are on average very high in all three cases, i.e., Korea–Japan, Japan–China, and China–Korea bilateral trade (see Table 3). They have remained relatively stable throughout the 2000s but modest changes are noted since the financial crisis. The index for consumer goods between Japan and China is low, although it has risen very sharply in recent years. In contrast, the index for consumer goods between Korea and Japan is lower than the index for

Table 3. **Intra-industry Trade among China, Japan and Korea: Grubel and Lloyd Index**

	Category	2000–04 Average	2005–09 Average	2010–14 Average
Japan–China	Parts and components	0.75	0.76	0.64
	Capital goods	0.98	0.88	0.81
	Consumer goods	0.10	0.19	0.82
Korea–China	Parts and components	0.64	0.60	0.33
	Capital goods	0.85	0.85	0.71
	Consumer goods	0.47	0.45	0.73
Korea–Japan	Parts and components	0.62	0.65	0.78
	Capital goods	0.46	0.60	0.59
	Consumer goods	0.62	0.92	0.57

Sources: UN COMTRADE Database.

parts and components — a reversal from the 2000s. However, one should note that the level of integration in Tables 2 and 3 do not necessarily measure the degree of horizontal integration in parts and components and capital goods. In a recent study, Lanz and Miroudot (2011) show that much of the trade in parts and components and capital goods takes the form of intra-firm trade between parent firms and their affiliates and between these affiliates.

Large shares of trade in different parts and components are also distinguished by technological and skill contents and used at various stages of the value chain between countries at different stages of development. These features suggest that more disaggregated data on the Grubel and Lloyd index would show an increase in vertical rather than horizontal integration in intra-industry trade among China, Japan, and Korea.

Although reliable data are not available, anecdotal evidence suggests that with the growth of foreign direct investment by Japan and Korea in China, intra-firm trade — between parent firms of the two countries and their affiliates in China — is likely to account for an increasing share of intra-industry trade between China on the one hand and Japan and Korea on the other.[7] More than any other enterprises, those heavily engaged in intra-firm trade will gain more from settling trade with their national currencies. Therefore, the growing share of intra-firm trade will help garner public support for the construction of the currency scheme in the region as a whole and among China, Japan, and Korea in particular.

2.5. Financial Openness

Government control of financial markets and the capital account together with currency inconvertibility has been and will continue to stand in the way of currency internationalization in China, Korea, and ASEAN-5. As shown in the subsequent sections, following the Chinese strategy, the new currency system proposed in this chapter explores the possibility of internationalization in a heavily regulated financial system before transiting to a more liberalized regime over time.

Since the early 2000, Korea has made a great deal of progress in developing a deregulated and open financial regime. As shown in the next section, China has come a long way from a relatively tightly controlled financial regime of the pre-2008 crisis period. Departing from its long standing policy of gradual reform in the past, the statement from the Third Plenary Session of the 18th Communist Party of China Central Committee has affirmed its plans to accelerate interest rate liberalization and capital account convertibility. Still, one should not undermine the challenge China faces in opening its capital and financial markets that have served the country's government-led growth well for the past several decades.

ASEAN has launched a long-term plan to liberalize and integrate financial markets and deregulate capital account transactions of the member countries, to be completed by around 2020. As proposed, there is no reason why all members can join the currency scheme before the target year.

Changes in East Asia's trade pattern and structure suggest that there is considerable room for deeper trade integration through an expansion of intra-regional trade in East Asia. Proliferation of FTAs and vertical

---

[7]However, the share of intra-firm trade in total manufactured exports was relatively small — only 10 percent in 2007 in Japan. See Lanz and Miroudot (2011).

structure of intra-industry trade are expected to help promote wider use of national currencies for trade invoicing and settlement, which could in turn speed up trade integration. At the same time if the scheme creates and builds up market pressure for domestic financial reform among the participating countries, it will also serve as a catalyst for harnessing regional cooperation for financial market integration.

3. Progress in the Internationalization of the Renminbi

China's financial markets are largely closed to foreign lenders and borrowers and its currency is not convertible. Yet, given the sheer size of its economy and its growing share in global trade, there is little doubt that the renminbi will emerge as East Asia's dominant currency and eventually attain global reserve currency status. As the second largest economy in the world, it may have a greater stake in global rather than regional integration at the level of ASEAN+3, but it also has interest in forging deeper economic relations with ASEAN, Japan, and Korea.[8] Moreover, regional currency scheme will expand the use of the renminbi beyond the limits dictated by the status of China's lack of financial openness and capital account convertibility.

Renminbi internationalization — understandably a long-term process — could reduce East Asia's reliance on the US dollar and make Asian currencies more flexible *vis-à-vis* the dollar. In March 2009, Zhou Xiaochuan, the governor of the People's Bank of China (PBC), spoke of reforming the international monetary system. He suggested introducing an international reserve currency, which, unlike the US dollar, could remain disconnected from individual nations and is able to prevail stability in the long run. Since then, China has made a tremendous effort

---

[8]Covering the period before the 2008 global financial crisis, Park (2010) and Park and Song (2011) show that there was a reasonable prospect for the renminbi to become a regional medium of exchange and even an anchor currency for a group of East Asian economies — ASEAN-10, Korea, Taiwan POC, and Hong Kong SAR. Since 2008, changes in trade relations and financial markets in the region appear to have further improved its position to become an international currency.

to internationalize renminbi (RMB), including facilitating its use in the international financial markets.

Further progress in renminbi internationalization, however, requires China to open access of its renminbi assets to non-residents, which implies capital account liberalization. Given the elevated global financial uncertainties since the 2008 crisis and excess liquidity swirling around in the global economy, the Chinese monetary authorities apparently came to the conclusion that rapid progress in capital account liberalization was undesirable and could even be destabilizing since China's domestic financial institutions have yet to become more efficient and stable to compete in the global environment.

China's response was to shift the focus to trade settlement in renminbi, instead of renminbi internationalization. It then opened windows to non-residents to access renminbi assets as necessary to keep the demand for renminbi alive. At the same time, it made steady progress to deregulate capital account transactions to facilitate the second stage of renminbi internationalization.

3.1. Renminbi as a Currency of Settlement

In April 2009, RMB took a big step towards a settlement currency. The pilot program of RMB settlement of cross-border trade transactions was launched by the State Council of China on the 56th Meeting of the State Council Standing Committee, with its intents to promote economic and trade ties between China and neighboring countries. The program allowed exporters and importers in Shanghai and four cities of Guangdong Province, namely Guangzhou, Shenzhen, Zhuhai, and Dongguan, to settle cross-border trade deals with Hong Kong, Macau, and ASEAN in RMB. Shanghai first initiated its RMB settlement business of cross-border trade in July 2009. The program soon expanded to 20 provinces, autonomous regions, and municipalities, and by June 2010, their operation spread to all other countries. The eligible transactions were also enlarged to include not only trade of goods but also trade of services, and other current account transactions.

All companies domiciled in those 20 regions were allowed to conduct RMB settlement for imports. However, RMB settlement for exports was

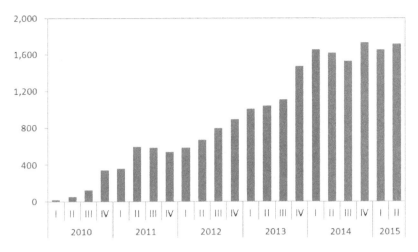

Figure 5.   Renminbi Settlement for Cross-border Trade
(Unit: In Billions of Renminbi)

Sources: CEIC.

still regulated, with only 365 eligible pilot enterprises. In October 2010, the PBC added more companies to the eligible pilot enterprises list, increasing the number to 67,359. In August 2011, the geographical coverage of cross-border trade was extended to the entire nation. In March 2012, the PBC allowed each and every company qualified for international trade activities to conduct cross-border export settlement in RMB to meet market demand and make foreign trade more free and convenient. Since then, all restrictions on trade settlement in RMB have been lifted.

The accumulated volume of China's cross-border trade settlement in renminbi under current accounts reached RMB10.2 trillion (US$1.7 trillion) by the end of 2013 (see Figure 5). The share of renminbi trade settlement in China's total international trade saw a six-fold increase from 3.2 percent in 2010 to 18 percent in 2013.[9] Yet, the use of the RMB has stalled since the beginning of 2014, indicating that it may have plateaued under the current level of China's development and the current status of its financial market.

---

[9] In value basis.

3.2. Renminbi Settlement Services and Interbank Market[10]

Solid foundation has been built for conducting the clearing services for RMB settlement. Hong Kong started the RMB settlement clearing operation at an early stage and has been the premier offshore RMB business center. Since 2004, banks in Hong Kong have been carrying out residents' personal RMB activities, even before the initiation of the RMB settlement program. In June 2009, the PBC and the Hong Kong Monetary Authority (HKMA) have renewed previously signed 2003 Memorandum of Co-operation on RMB clearing services. Bank of China (Hong Kong) has been the sole RMB clearing bank. In December 2013, the volume of RMB trade settlement in Hong Kong hit RMB470 billion, accounting for 81.2% of total RMB trade settlement.[11]

Macau also has provided RMB clearing services by the Macau branch of Bank of China (BOC). Singapore and Taiwan started RMB clearing services and became primary offshore RMB financial centers. In August 2012, China and Taiwan signed the Memorandum of Understanding (MOU) agreeing to establish a currency clearing mechanism. The PBC authorized the Taipei branch of Bank of China to be the RMB clearing bank in December 2012 and signed Clearing Agreement on RMB Business with the Taipei branch of BOC in January 2013. In February 2013, the PBC announced authorizing the Singapore branch of Industrial and Commercial Bank of China (ICBC) to be the RMB clearing bank in Singapore. China began renminbi settlement of overseas direct investment in January 2011, and in October of the same year, it allowed domestic banks to operate overseas renminbi loan services.[12]

Furthermore, China has expanded the direct trading of RMB with non-major-reserve currencies. In August 2010, the trading between RMB and Malaysian ringgit was launched in the interbank foreign exchange

---

[10] More recent developments have been explained in Chapter 5.
[11] Hong Kong SAR hosts the largest pool of renminbi liquidity outside Mainland China. Banks and other financial institutions in Hong Kong SAR now offer a full range of renminbi financial products, including certificate of deposits, renminbi stocks, renminbi insurance policies, renminbi futures, and "dual currencies, dual stocks" that were denominated in both renminbi and Hong Kong dollar.
[12] See the People's Bank of China (2011b).

market by China Foreign Exchange Trade System (CFETS) to promote the bilateral trade, cross-border settlement, and overall to reduce exchange costs. Ringgit was the first emerging market currency traded in China's interbank market. From November 2010, Russian ruble also started to trade directly with RMB on the interbank market and the Russian Moscow Interbank Currency Exchange (MICEX) officially launched the trading of the RMB against the ruble on its market in December 2010. Later in December 2011, the direct trading of RMB against the Thai baht was launched on the interbank market in Yunnan Province. RMB began to trade directly against Japanese yen since June 2012. By April 2013, the CFETS announced to launch direct trading between the RMB and Australian dollar on the interbank market. Currently, nine currencies are permitted to be traded in the interbank foreign exchange market.[13]

3.3. Interbank Market for the Renminbi

In July 2007, the first issuance of RMB-denominated bond, the so-called Dim Sum bond, was launched in Hong Kong by the Asian Development Bank (ADB). Since then, Chinese financial institutions were given approval to issue RMB-denominated bonds in Hong Kong. The Chinese Finance Ministry issued sovereign bonds denominated in RMB for the first time in September 2009 in Hong Kong, helping to construct the yield curve of the offshore RMB bond market. The offshore RMB bond market has grown rapidly since July 2010, as the Clearing Agreement for RMB business was amended to facilitate the development of RMB asset management and insurance products. Departing from Hong Kong, RMB-denominated bond with an amount of RMB2 billion was also issued in London in April 2012 for the first time by HSBC.

China has steadily opened onshore financial markets to foreign investors. It allowed foreigners to invest and trade in the domestic securities market for the first time in 2002 by launching the qualified foreign institutional investor (QFII) program. Only licensed foreign investors have

---

[13]The US dollar, euro, Japanese yen, Hong Kong dollar, British pound sterling, Malaysian ringgit, Russian ruble, Australian dollar, and Canadian dollar can be traded. The Thai baht can also be traded, but only in the province of Yunnan.

been allowed to buy and sell equities and bonds in China's stock exchanges in Shanghai and Shenzhen. Since then, China has increased the amount of quota and as of January 2014, a total of 235 foreign institutional investors and US$51.4 billion quota have been approved under the QFII program.[14] By June 2015, this amount has risen to US$75.5 billion.

The renminbi qualified foreign institutional investors (RQFII) scheme launched in December 2011 permits renminbi fund investments in China's domestic financial assets, whereas the QFII scheme is reserved for US dollar-denominated investments. The investment quota for RQFII rose to RMB382.7 billion for 129 institutions in May 2015. Also, foreign central banks and renminbi clearing banks outside China have been allowed to invest their renminbi funds in China's interbank bond market since August 2010. Their RMB funds shall come from currency cooperation between central banks, cross-border trades, and investment in RMB business. In March 2013, the PBC published the Notice on Issues Related to Investment in the Inter-bank Bond Market by Qualified Foreign Institutional Investors, allowing QFIIs to apply to invest in the interbank bond market. Prior to that, QFIIs can only access the exchange bond market.

3.4. Renminbi as a Reserve Currency

To improve short-term liquidity conditions and to promote bilateral trade, the PBC signed the bilateral local currency swap agreement with Bank of Korea in December 2008. It was established on top of the existing arrangement under CMIM. Since then, China's bilateral local currency swap expanded further. By June 2015, China signed bilateral renminbi–local currency swap agreements with central banks or monetary authorities of 30 countries and regions, amounting to RMB3.0 trillion (see Table 4).

Since the relaxation of investments in China's interbank bond market in 2010, a growing number of foreign central banks have begun to invest in China's government bonds — to hold as part of their foreign reserves. In December 2011, the People's Bank of China announced that the Bank of

---

[14] In October 2011, China allowed renminbi-denominated direct investment in China for overseas investors in order to facilitate the direct investment and the People's Bank of China (2011a) issued the rules on settlement of renminbi-denominated foreign direct investment, stipulating that banks start to provide settlement services.

Table 4. Bilateral Currency Swap Agreements Negotiated by China

Number	Country	Amount (RMB Billion)	Date
1	Belarus	20	March 11, 2009
2	Argentina	70	April 2, 2009
3	New Zealand	25	April 18, 2011
4	Uzbekistan	0.7	April 19, 2011
5	Kazakhstan	7	June 13, 2011
6	South Korea	360	October 26, 2011
		(180)	(December 12, 2008)
7	Hong Kong	400	November 22, 2011
		(200)	(January 20, 2009)
8	Thailand	70	December 22, 2011
9	Pakistan	10	December 23, 2011
10	United Arab Emirates	35	January 17, 2012
11	Malaysia	180	February 8, 2012
		(80)	(February 8, 2009)
12	Turkey	10	February 21, 2012
13	Mongolia	10	March 20, 2012
		(5)	(May 6, 2011)
14	Australia	200	March 22, 2012
15	Ukraine	15	June 26, 2012
16	Singapore	300	March 7, 2013
		(150)	(July 23, 2010)
17	Brazil	190	March 26, 2013
18	United Kingdom	200	June 22, 2013
19	Hungary	10	September 9, 2013
20	Iceland	3.5	September 11, 2013
			(June 9, 2010)
21	Albania	2	September 12, 2013
22	Indonesia	100	October 1, 2013
			(March 23, 2009)
23	European Central Bank	350	October 9, 2013
24	Switzerland	150	July 14, 2014
25	Sri Lanka	10	September 16, 2014
26	Qatar	35	November 3, 2014
27	Canada	200	November 8, 2014
28	Suriname	1	March 18, 2015
29	South Africa	30	April 10, 2015
30	Chile	22	May 25, 2015

Notes: The numbers in the parentheses refer to initial swaps and the date.
Sources: The People's Bank of China.

Japan would invest in China's government bonds. In April 2013, Reserve Bank of Australia announced its decision to invest up to 5 percent of their foreign reserves in renminbi through the Australian Chamber of Commerce in Shanghai. It was reported that Chile, Malaysia, and Nigeria also hold renminbi bonds as part of their foreign reserves.[15]

3.5. The Shanghai Pilot Free Trade Zone

China established the Shanghai Pilot Free Trade Zone in September 2013. In its effort to support the development of the free trade zone, the People's Bank of China (2014) announced the general principles to apply to its operations and development. One of them is continuing reform and innovation, and leading the way in experimentation to promote cross-border use of the renminbi and move toward capital account convertibility, market-based interest rate reform, and foreign exchange administration reform.

The central bank allowed the banking institutions located in Shanghai to process directly cross-border renminbi settlement for current account transactions and foreign direct investment. Also, financial institutions and non-financial companies located in Shanghai can borrow renminbi fund from overseas.[16] Further measures are expected to be adopted in the free trade zone to speed up internationalization of the renminbi.

3.6. Policies to Promote Investments in RMB-denominated Financial Assets

China has been making steady progress in promoting investments in financial assets denominated in RMB as a mean to increase RMB demand. In this regard, Hong Kong has served well as an offshore RMB hub in line with the expectation noted in China's Twelfth Five-Year Plan for Economic and Social Development. In particular, it supported the development of Hong Kong as an international asset management center via the

---

[15] *Financial Times* (April 25, 2013).
[16] However, the borrowed money must not be used for investment in securities or derivatives.

establishment of cross-border RMB trade settlement. By now, it hosts the largest pool of RMB liquidity outside Mainland China. Banks and other financial institutions in Hong Kong offer a full range of RMB financial products, including certificate of deposits, RMB stocks, RMB insurance policies, RMB futures, and "dual currencies, dual stocks" that were denominated in both RMB and Hong Kong dollar.

In June 2012, the HKMA installed a facility to provide RMB liquidity to Authorized Institutions participating in RMB business (Participating AIs) in Hong Kong using the currency swap arrangement with the PBC. The Participating AIs' facility was reinforced in July 2013, with the role of providing one-day funds beyond its existing role of providing one-week RMB funds. The HKMA also disclosed plans to introduce a CNH Hong Kong Interbank Offered Rate (HIBOR) fixing, which should further support development of the offshore RMB-denominated bond market by providing a benchmark for pricing floating rate bonds in June 2013. Also, the newly established "HKMA CMU Central Bank Placement Coordinating Window" provided the tendering platform for the successful issuance of offshore RMB sovereign bonds in Hong Kong in June 2012 and June 2013.

In addition to the RQFII which relates to portfolio investment flows, a pilot scheme relating to cross-border banking flows were initiated from January 2013. Under the scheme, the eligible financial institutions in Hong Kong are allowed to provide RMB-denominated loans to entities in Mainland China specifically for construction and development in Qianhai.

Another key scheme which links the offshore market in Hong Kong and onshore market in Mainland China is a Pilot Scheme for Three Kinds of Eligible Institutions Outside of the Mainland to Invest in China's Interbank Bond Market, which was launched in 2010. Under the scheme, foreign central banks and monetary authorities, the RMB clearing banks in Hong Kong and Macau, and banks outside Mainland China participating cross-border trade settlement transaction can invest their RMB fund in the interbank bond market of Mainland China. In spite of the launching of the scheme, by the end of April 2015, the foreign banks secured only 2 percent (a total of 535 RMB billion) of total RMB-denominated government bond in the inter-bank bond market, according to China Central Depository & Clearing (CCDC).

Furthermore, after allowing RMB-denominated direct investment in China for foreign investors in 2011, the State Administration of Foreign Exchange (SAFE) simplified regulations covering foreign direct investment in May 2013.

In July 2013, the PBC issued the Notice on Simplifying the Procedures for Cross-border RMB Business and Improving the Relevant Policies. It simplified the cross-border RMB business procedures under the current account and streamlined the cross-border clearing business of RMB bankcard accounts. Also, it standardized the overseas RMB loan business by domestic non-financial institutions, the issuance of RMB-denominated bonds in overseas markets, and so forth.

4. Objectives and the Potential Size of the Currency Scheme in East Asia

4.1. Objectives

The combined GDP of the economies of East Asia including ASEAN, China, Japan, and Korea — ASEAN+3 — is already as large as that of the United States. East Asia is home to a number of international financial centers. It has a large number of growing domestic financial markets linked with one another more closely than before. In 2010, ASEAN+3 accounted for more than 25 percent of global trade, yet the shares of the two major currencies — the yen and the renminbi in the region — in total global trade payments were about 2.5 and 0.24 percent, respectively, whereas their shares in total global trade were 5 and 11 percent (Auboin 2012).

If East Asian countries are serious about addressing the mismatch between trade and payment, constructing a regional scheme for using some of the regional currencies including non-convertible ones for trade settlement could prove to be an effective strategy for reducing their dependence on the US dollar, enhancing flexibility of their currencies against the US dollar, and dampening any financial spillovers emanating from advanced economies.

In addition, such a regional currency arrangement will also help internationalize some of the non-convertible currencies, thereby speeding up trade and financial integration in the region at the same time. The scheme is also expected to provide fresh impetus to support various regional free trade negotiations underway and revive cooperation for financial integration within the framework of ASEAN+3 that has been stalled by global financial instability and stagnation.

Among the currencies of East Asian countries, the yen is a full-fledged reserve currency. As shown in the preceding section, China has put into effect a number of measures for deregulating capital account transactions and limited opening of domestic financial markets for foreign investments. Although they are hardly adequate for what are required for full-fledged currency internationalization, it has now advanced too much to retreat from the pilot program: it is expected to continue to move forward with financial reform. Korea has made several attempts to internationalize its currency, but Korea failed each time because it did not have the will or political support for the requisite institutional and policy reform.[17]

At the 12th ASEAN Summit in January 2007, the member countries affirmed their commitment to create the ASEAN Economic Community by 2015 and "to transform ASEAN into a region with free movement of goods, services, investment, [and] skilled labor, and freer flow of capital" (ASEAN 2008). To achieve this ambitious goal in the financial sector, ASEAN has drawn up "plans for capital account liberalization (CAL) and financial services liberalization (FSL) in the ASEAN banking sector, together with institutional and policy reforms and an ASEAN framework for policy coordination and mutual assistance over 2011–2020" (ADB 2013, 1).

The probability of success of the proposed multilateral currency settlement scheme would be higher, if it begins with the currencies of China, Japan, and Korea, largely because they are major trade partners to each other. We assume that some of the ASEAN-5 member states could join the system from the beginning on a voluntary basis. Over time, the currency arrangement could increase the number of participating countries as well as the scope of coverage of settlement, to include, eventually, capital account transactions. However, use of national currencies would need to be a gradual process, with stability concerns fully addressed at each stage.

In constructing the scheme, this study envisions a multilateral arrangement in which the participating countries agree to use not only

---

[17] See Kim and Suh (2011) on Korea's internationalization of the won.

Table 5.   Use of National Currencies in Trade Settlement[1]

(Unit: %)

	Korea–China[2]	Korea–Japan[2]	China–Japan[3]
US dollar	96.1	46.4	52.4
Renminbi	0.5	—	0.4
Euro	0.7	0.6	0.4
Yen	0.7	48.4	43.9
Won	1.9	4.5	—
Hong Kong dollar	0.02	0.0001	1.6

Notes: [1]Trade settlement refers to the sum of exports and imports.
[2]Average, January–March 2015.
[3]May 2012.
Sources: Bank of Korea.

their own currencies but also those of others as vehicle currencies in bilateral trade settlements with other partners. For instance, Chinese traders could make payments for their imports from Korea with any one of the participating currencies. As shown in Table 5, more than 40 percent of bilateral trade between Korea and Japan and between China and Japan were settled by the yen in recent years. In comparison, similar shares for the renminbi were paltry at 0.5 percent with Korea and 0.4 percent with Japan. None of the yen, renminbi, and won was used in trade with third countries as a vehicle currency.

At the country level, the new currency system brings several benefits to the participating countries similar to those enjoyed by countries with an internationalized currency, which include lower transaction costs, reduced exchange rate risk, and the ability to issue international debt in their own currencies. However, the participating countries will have to bear substantial costs too, as they are exposed to a number of risks in addition to those difficulties that countries with an internationalized currency often encounter, such as complications of monetary management and straining the domestic financial system's ability to handle increased volatility and large shifts in portfolio flows.[18]

---

[18] For a comprehensive discussion on benefits and cost, see Maziad *et al.* (2011).

A few challenges will need to be addressed. Since traders are free to choose the currency they prefer, they may discriminate against non-convertible currencies in favor of a currency like the yen in their trade settlement. The onus will therefore be on the non-convertible currency members to make their currencies more attractive to traders as a vehicle for financial investments as well as for trade settlement.

Another is the problem of clearing imbalances of currency outflows and inflows stemming from trade deficits or surpluses of the participating countries. If one member runs a persistent deficit on its trade account, then the system may come under strain in the absence of an adjustment mechanism that could control the flows. This problem could be of manageable proportions, if capping on the use of national currencies for settling import bills could be imposed during the initial phase (years) of this arrangement.

A third is the downside risk associated with changes in the imbalances in currency flows, which could create opportunities for currency speculation, increasing the volatility of capital flows and hence the bilateral exchange rates of the member countries. These problems, as discussed in the following section, could be mitigated if the scheme institutes a currency swaps arrangement through which short-term liquidity could be made available to the members suffering from temporary liquidity shortage of a particular currency. In any event, at the initial stage, such position taking will be limited as currencies will be tied to real transactions.

4.2. Potential Size

Based on the 2014 data, and assuming that all trade settlements take place in respective national currencies — export receipts are received in importing country's currencies — a multilateral agreement that covers only trade settlement in national currencies results in a net outflow of national currencies equivalent to US$146 billion for the nine economies as a whole, as shown in Table 6.

The largest amount will be the use of the Hong Kong dollar, amounting to US$166 billion, followed by renminbi, equivalent to US$41 billion. Korea and Singapore, each of which would have a current account surplus against the countries listed in Table 6, accumulate other Asian

Beyond the Dollar and the Euro

Table 6. National Currency Outflows from the Multilateral Trade Settlement Scheme in National Currencies in 2014

(Unit: In Millions of US Dollars)

	Export to									
	HK	China	Japan	Korea	Indonesia	Malaysia	Philippines	Thailand	Singapore	Net
Hong Kong		290,287	16,914	8,006	2,577	3,739	2,983	7,527	7,761	339,795
China	363,088		149,410	100,335	39,060	46,355	23,474	34,293	48,912	804,928
Japan	37,804	124,986		50,488	14,665	13,958	9,812	31,105	20,970	303,787
Korea	27,256	145,288	32,184		11,361	7,583	10,032	7,599	23,750	265,053
Indonesia	2,778	17,606	23,166	10,621		9,759	3,888	5,830	16,807	90,454
Malaysia	11,314	28,223	25,277	8,572	9,706		3,682	12,308	33,263	132,343
Philippines	5,594	8,034	13,919	2,532	759	1,161		2,352	4,454	38,804
Thailand	12,610	25,084	21,821	4,520	9,510	12,764	5,868		10,455	102,633
Singapore	45,109	51,501	16,746	16,698	38,370	48,998	6,871	15,047		239,340
Net	505,552	691,009	299,436	201,772	126,007	144,317	66,611	116,061	166,371	2,317,137

Table 6.   *(Continued)*

									Net
Hong Kong	−72,801	−20,890	−19,250	−201	−7,575	−2,611	−5,083	−37,347	−165,758
China		24,424	−44,953	21,454	18,133	15,441	9,209	−2,589	41,118
Japan			18,304	−8,501	−11,319	−4,107	9,285	4,224	7,886
Korea				739	−989	7,500	3,079	7,052	17,382
Indonesia					53	3,129	−3,680	−21,563	−22,061
Malaysia						2,521	−457	−15,735	−13,671
Philippines							−3,516	−2,417	−5,934
Thailand								−4,593	−4,593
Singapore									
Net	−72,801	3,534	−45,899	13,491	−1,697	21,873	8,836	−72,969	−145,631

Notes: [1]Negative amounts represent inflows into the export recipient country.
[2]Adjusted for re-exports through Hong Kong.
Sources: Authors' estimation.

currencies equivalent to US$46 billion and US$73 billion, respectively. In reality, the actual amounts of the net outflows are likely to be much smaller than the maximum figures shown in Table 6, suggesting that the total amount of the imbalances between the three countries would be of a volume manageable for clearance.

5. Structure of the System

The proposed system is built on a set of multilateral agreements among the participating countries on an institutional and operational framework that include:

 (i) convertibility of national currencies of the participating countries received as export payments;
 (ii) a clearing and settlement mechanism, involving the designation of clearing banks;
(iii) the creation of interbank foreign exchange markets for direct trading in some of the members;
(iv) investment vehicles for exporters with non-national currencies received from their trading partners; and
 (v) an adjustment mechanism for imbalances in currency flows between trade surplus and deficit countries.

Agreement on these five points is critical to the success of the system as they are designed to alleviate some of the constraints on use of non-convertible currencies.

5.1. Convertibility

In this currency arrangement, exporters and importers decide on the choice of currency for their transactions. To ensure competition among the participating currencies, national governments should not intervene to dictate the choice to be in favor of particular currencies. Importers will favor use of their national currencies, but it is a different matter to exporters. In choosing a settlement currency, they would consider, among other things, changes in the expected exchange rates of the currencies of their trading partners, transactions and hedging costs, and, most of all, convertibility into their own or other reserve currencies such as the US dollar.

Exporters are likely to prefer payments of their receipts in yen rather than other non-convertible currencies including the renminbi unless their full convertibility is guaranteed. Their preference for reserve currencies will be even stronger if they import inputs for their exports from non-member countries, which may demand payments in reserve currencies. Exporters may have still fewer incentives to accept non-convertible currencies if they are not allowed to invest their export proceeds in domestic financial assets denominated in their trading partners' currencies.

Two of the keys to the successful launching and expansion of the currency scheme will therefore be sustaining stability of the exchange rates and ensuring access of traders to domestic financial markets of the non-convertible currencies. We turn to these issues below.

5.2. Clearing and Settlement

A well-organized multicurrency clearing and settlement system offering services in all participating currencies would be crucial for the efficiency of the operation of the currency scheme. The initial construction of such a system will be the most difficult hurdle the architects of the currency system will have to deal with, as they are faced with unevenly developed national clearing and settlement arrangements and different business practices across the member countries. These differences could also be a major source of systemic risk and inefficiency.[19]

The clearing and settlement system is built on a network of clearing banks established throughout the participating countries. These clearing

---

[19] Even in the early 2000s when the European Union had already developed into a highly integrated region, a 2001 study on cross-border clearing and settlement arrangements in the European Union by the Giovannini group for the European Commission found that cross-border transactions within Europe are far more complex, are hindered by a number of significant barriers, and are much more costly than domestic transactions. Inefficiencies in clearing and settlement represent the most primitive and thus most important barrier to integrated financial markets in Europe.

banks provide local banks with diversified clearing services, including settlement accounts, deposit and withdrawal of banknotes, remittance, foreign exchange and bonds settlement in all participating currencies. In the process, they would manage counterparty risk and guarantee contractual performance by playing the role of central counterparty and serve as settlement agents for and intermediaries between local clearing banks and their respective central banks.

5.3. Interbank Foreign Exchange Markets

The convertibility guarantee and an efficient clearing and settlement system would be critical to the scheme in establishing its credibility at the early stage of its development. However, equally important would be the need to complement the scheme by creating the interbank foreign exchange markets for the participating currencies to facilitate their direct trading.

At the initial stage, state-owned banks or other designated non-bank financial institutions could serve as market makers to provide liquidity and to set and control transactions costs to facilitate creation of the markets onshore and offshore.[20] Interbank markets for the renminbi and the yen are already in operation in both Shanghai and Tokyo. Other members will need to make preparations for creating the onshore and offshore markets for their currencies.

5.4. Investment Vehicles

Each member country may create an investment vehicle reserved exclusively for exporters of other member countries to invest their holdings of the country's currency. The demand for the instruments issued by the vehicles could be controlled by adjusting the return on these assets. The most basic instrument would be deposits offered by the clearing banks.

---

[20] In 1996 Korea opened a won/yen market, but closed it less than a year later because of the lack of liquidity and high costs of transactions compared with the won/US dollar and yen/US dollar markets.

5.5. Adjustments of Imbalances of Holdings of National Currencies

Trade account developments would differ from country to county and the participating countries may run deficit or surplus in their bilateral trade with other members. The new scheme faces the problem of managing imbalances in national currency outflows. As shown in Table 6, for example, China has been running deficits in its bilateral trade with both Japan and Korea. China will then experience a continuing outflow of renminbi, which will be absorbed by the surplus countries. Unless these imbalances are managed in a way that can prevent an excessive accumulation of a particular currency outside of its issuer to sustain stability of the foreign exchange markets, the scheme will come under strain.

It is difficult to conjecture the effects of the national currency scheme on trade account balances of the participating countries. The scheme may, other things being equal, stimulate imports to the extent that importers can use their national currencies, but the actual increase will also depend on exporters' choice of currency for settlement. This feature of the system could interfere or help with adjustments of trade imbalances among the members by increasing the volatility of exchange rates, exacerbating speculation in the foreign exchange markets, and complicating the conduct of monetary policy. Therefore, a protracted one-sided trade deficit or surplus will need to be addressed through an adjustment mechanism that is agreeable to the members.

Although importers are not — and should not be — subject to any restrictions in using a national currency, a limit could be set initially on the use of each currency for trade settlement at the country level to prevent excessive accumulation of the deficit country's currency. For example, if Korea runs a larger bilateral deficit in its trade with Japan, Japanese banks (whose customers are the Japanese exporters) may end up holding more Korean won than they desire. The monetary authorities of Japan and Korea will then agree to a bilateral adjustment mechanism to clear the excessive accumulation of Korean won in Japan. If the volume of the actual settlement exceeds the limit, then the excess could be settled by the yen or other reserve currencies such as the US dollar or the euro.

To be more specific, suppose that Japan and Korea agree to settle 50 percent of Korea's imports from Japan in Korean won. If the actual amount of the won settlement exceeded the limit, the difference would be adjusted *ex post* in terms of the yen or the US dollar as a "rebalancing" currency, through a clearing mechanism set up by the two countries' central banks.

The participating countries could also entertain a more gradual approach for adjustment. Suppose Japan accumulates 100 million units of Korean won at the end of the year due to an increase in trade imbalance. A limit could first be set at 100 million units, and then increase to two times 100 million units. During the second year, Japan would be expected to exchange any amount, including zero, in excess of 100 million units of the Korean won with the US dollar. For any amount in excess of three times 100 million units, Japan would be required to exchange with the US dollar with Korea such that the total amount does not exceed three times the base year's trade imbalance.[21]

6. Benefits and Risks

6.1. Benefits

Although it is fully convertible, the yen has not been as widely used as a full-fledged reserve currency. Most of Japan's exports are still invoiced in US dollar. As the share of ASEAN+3 in its total trade continues to grow as shown in Figure 3 (see page 16), Japan will benefit more than other countries from joining the currency scheme. This is because the yen has a competitive edge — exporters are likely to favor it — over the other cur-

---

[21] One can extend this arrangement to cover all ASEAN+3 countries and allow any country to exchange bilateral excesses with any one among the selected currencies with any country that has space and is willing. In other words, extending the above example, country A can exchange 100 million unit of country B's currency with country C with country D's currency if the latter's holding of country B's currency is within three times the originally set limit. The logic behind this approach is to allow countries to adjust holding other country's currencies gradually. This will lead to greater use of the selected currencies within ASEAN+3, and thus reduce overall reliance on the US dollar and euro.

rencies for trade settlement. More importantly, if most ASEAN-5 countries sign on, Japan will find it in their interest to go along with them.

Taking advantage of its vast market for regional exporters and importers as leverage, China could take the lead in promoting the new currency scheme. The benefits to China would be sizeable, as the scheme will help broaden its regional base as a launching pad for renminbi globalization. The new currency scheme will also provide some impetus for China to speed up the pace of renminbi internationalization by breaking the impasse on capital account liberalization.

Korea has taken a few steps towards internationalizing its currency. It has established bilateral currency swap arrangements with China, Japan, Malaysia, Indonesia, and the United Arab Emirates in recent years and plans to negotiate similar arrangements with other countries. As a highly open economy that is extensively integrated with the global economy, Korea realizes that it has no choice but to open its financial industries and make the won convertible. Participation in the currency scheme may help Korea's policy makers garner domestic support to — and speed up — capital account liberalization and currency convertibility.

For other countries, the benefit would be equally substantial. It would boost confidence in their currencies and allow them to hold relatively fewer reserves in convertible currencies than before. The total amount of foreign exchange reserves held by these countries could be smaller as the use of other currencies for current account settlement will require a smaller buffer, and the inter-changeability of these currencies implies *de facto* a pooling of foreign exchange reserves in convertible currencies.

Finally, the new currency arrangement will strengthen regional capacity to absorb external shocks. As the acceptance of these currencies grows within the bloc, one could expect less volatility among bilateral exchange rates of the East Asian currencies, and greater flexibility of the weighted average East Asian currencies against the euro and the US dollar.

6.2. Relative Advantages

If the experience with forming the CMIM is any guide, constructing a multinational arrangement involving a number of currencies would require an enormous amount of time for negotiations on the details of the scheme among the participating countries. Furthermore, the benefits could not be easily gauged while the risks could be magnified. For this reason, many detractors would not see the benefits of such a scheme.

They would argue that if any country wishes to internationalize its currency, all it has to do is to open its financial markets, remove restrictions on capital account transactions, and make its currency convertible. In particular, they would question the rationale for the participation of China, and more so of Japan, of which yen is a full-fledged reserve currency.

While these objections deserve merit, they overlook a critical advantage that individual attempts cannot deliver. In internationalizing their currencies, emerging economies will find it more expedient, but much less risky and less costly, if they work with other countries in a multilateral framework where the participating members agree to use — and construct requisite infrastructure and a framework for policy cooperation — their national currencies for trade settlement than when they pursue it individually.

Given that the internationalization is essentially a market-driven process, it is uncertain how successful individual attempts will be, even if they are preceded by the reform satisfying most of the preconditions. In a cooperative framework it is at least assured — and expected by market expects — that their currencies will be acceptable for settlement of trade at least among the participating countries, thereby overcoming some of the teething problems, while reaping the gains from the network externality.

In addition, by participating in a multilateral currency scheme, emerging economies could reduce severity of some of the difficulties currency internationalization entails, such as complicating monetary management and increasing the volatility of capital flows. This benefit could be realized by instituting a mutual liquidity support system and setting up a common capital control regime. Finally, participation in the currency scheme may provide justification and build up peer pressure for an extensive financial reform in emerging economies that would find it difficult to implement on their own.

Japan's participation will be crucial to the success of the scheme. As the only member holding a reserve currency, its involvement will enhance not only credibility and stability but also confidence of other participating members. It may also help the participating countries to avoid the strategic misjudgments Japan made in internationalizing the yen.

Although it is the world's third largest economy, Japan has failed to expand the role of the yen in the global trading and monetary system with the share of the Japanese economy in the world. According to Takagi (2011, 83), "By the end of 2003 ... it was clear that any further attempt to internationalize the yen ... would be futile without a fundamental change in the economic might of Japan or major cooperation efforts among Asian countries to promote the role of the yen in the region."

Japan has a large stake in a vast and growing export market of East Asia. Joining the scheme will help expand the scope of the yen as a regional settlement currency and thereby regain its export market share — which has been declining — and strengthen its role in deepening regional trade and financial market integration in East Asia. Most important of all, as a reserve currency country, Japan could enjoy the vantage point where it could dictate the terms for settling its bilateral trade with other participating countries with non-convertible currencies.

As for China, having so far managed successfully its internationalization program, one might argue that the country will not have any incentives to deviate from its independent strategy. That may be true, but over time the increase in renminbi circulation outside the country is likely to slow down unless China is prepared to overhaul its financial system to allow foreign holders of renminbi easy access to its domestic financial markets and make the renminbi fully convertible. Furthermore, if China plans to consolidate the regional base of its currency, both Japan and Korea will have to use the renminbi more extensively for their trade settlement than they did in the past. The currency scheme could be one way of achieving that objective.

Although the Chinese authorities claim that they are deeply committed to financial liberalization and openness, they are also faced with a formidable domestic opposition against the internationalization scheme, which is viewed as a cover for an extensive financial market and capital account liberalization that China may not benefit from and certainly is not ready for — at least for now (Yu 2012).

China cannot internationalize its currency and retain a repressive financial regime at the same time. If the globalization of the renminbi is part of the vision of China as a global power, renminbi internationalization could serve as a banner under which parties of conflicting interests are brought together to create a deregulated financial system and its vision is realized.

6.3. Risks and Their Management

The participating countries will have to tolerate the same costs countries with an international currency have to bear. Use of one's currency outside its borders could become a source of complacency in the conduct of monetary policy. For example, a growing domestic imbalance could be financed by printing money as the usual market reaction may be absent.

In addition, they are exposed to other risks. To the extent that use of national currencies is limited to settlement of current account transactions, the incidence of speculative attack is relatively small and could be controlled. Even then, currency speculation could increase since currency traders can expect with some degree of certainty accumulation of one particular country against another from trade imbalance. As noted before, however, this pressure can be alleviated by introducing a mechanism for adjustment such as conversion into a fully convertible currency and fortifying it with currency swaps as short-term borrowing arrangements.

7. Concluding Remarks

Instability of the US dollar funding market that followed the 2008 global financial crisis has prompted China to consider ways of reducing its reliance on the US dollar through renminbi internationalization. Korea and Singapore secured access to a foreign exchange swap facility with the US Federal Reserve to ensure uninterrupted funding in the US dollar and to assure investors of their capacity to meet foreign exchange obligations. While these swap lines were critical to restoring currency stability in East Asian economies during the 2008 global financial crisis, they have further strengthened Asia's reliance on the US dollar as a reserve currency.

Over the long run, this situation is not tenable as economic activities in East Asian economies are unnecessarily disrupted by developments in the US dollar market beyond the trade and capital flow channels. Furthermore, it subjects these countries to US monetary policy that may not be optimal for their own economic situations. Each time there is uncertainty in the global financial market that leads to heightened risk aversion, East Asian economies will be at the mercy of changes in the US dollar funding market conditions, possibly forcing them to seek swap lines with the Federal Reserve. Moreover, to the extent most of the trade invoices and much of the cost are priced in US dollar, East Asian economies are reluctant to allow their currencies to instantly and fully adjust their value *vis-à-vis* the US dollar to any change in the external environment. This often leads to delayed clearance of imbalances.

China has already set the stage for use of national currencies in settling trade in the region. East Asia would find it more effective in reducing its reliance on the US dollar if more ASEAN+3 member states would emulate China's strategy for renminbi internationalization. This chapter argues that economic conditions are ripe for some of the ASEAN+3 members — in particular Korea and some of the ASEAN-5 member states — to join forces together with Japan and China to create a multinational currency arrangement where the currencies of these countries could be used for trade settlement.

The capital account regimes of these potential members still retain a large number of measures of capital control. Unless they are deregulated and the respective national currencies are made convertible, the new currency system would not be viable as a scheme for currency internationalization in the long run. However, in the meantime, the proposed scheme could go a long way to overcome some of the shortcomings of the current international monetary system (IMS) and help internationalize the RMB and a few other local currencies in the process. This chapter proposes that some of the market-supporting institutions need to be set up to support the new currency scheme. If these institutions do not work, they will at least build up pressure for capital account liberalization.

References

ASEAN (Association of Southeast Asian Nations) (2008). ASEAN Economic Community Blueprint. Jakarta: ASEAN Secretariat.

Asian Development Bank (2013). The Road to ASEAN Financial Integration: A Combined Study on Assessing the Financial Landscape and Formulating Milestones for Monetary and Financial Integration in ASEAN. Mandaluyong City, Philippines: Asian Development Bank.

Auboin, Marc (2012). Use of Currencies in International Trade: Any Changes in the Picture? Staff Working Paper No. ERSD-2012-10. Geneva: World Trade Organization.

Financial Times (April 25, 2013).

Grubel, Herbert G., and Peter J. Lloyd (1975). *Intra-Industry Trade: The Theory and Measurement of Internationally Trade in Differentiated Products*. London: Macmillan.

Kawai, Masahiro and Ganeshan Wignaraja (2013). *Patterns of Free Trade Areas in Asia. Policy Studies*, No. 65. Honolulu: East-West Center.

Kenen, Peter B. (2011). Currency Internationalization: An Overview. *BIS Papers*, No. 61, 9–18. Basel: Bank for International Settlements.

Kim, Kyungsoo and Young Kyung Suh (2011). Dealing with the Benefits and Costs of Internationalization of the Korean Won. BIS Papers, No. 61, 151–171. Basel: Bank for International Settlements.

Lanz, R. and S. Miroudot (2011). Intra-Firm Trade: Patterns, Determinants and Policy Implications. *OECD Trade Policy Papers*, No. 114. Paris: OECD Publishing.

Maziad, Samar, Pascal Farahmand, Shengzu Wang, Stephanie Segal, and Faisal Ahmed (2011). Internationalization of Emerging Market Currencies: A Balance between Risks and Rewards. IMF Staff Discussion Note No. 11/17. Washington, DC: International Monetary Fund.

Park, Yung Chul (2010). RMB Internationalization and Its Implications for Financial and Monetary Cooperation in East Asia. *China and World Economy*, 18(2): 1–21.

Park, Yung Chul and Chi-Young Song (2011). Renminbi Internationalization: Prospects and Implications for Economic Integration in East Asia. *Asian Economic Papers*, 10(3): 42–72.

People's Bank of China (2010). Notice of the People's Bank of China on Issues Concerning the Pilot Program on Investment in the Inter-bank Bond Market with RMB Funds by Three Types of Institution Including Overseas RMB Clearing Banks. PBC Document No. 217. Beijing: People's Bank of China.

People's Bank of China (2011a). Administrative Rules on Settlement of RMB-denominated Foreign Direct Investment. PBC Document No. 23. Beijing: People's Bank of China.

People's Bank of China (2011b). Guidelines of the People's Bank of China on RMB Loans of Domestic Banking Institutions for Overseas Projects. PBC Document No. 255. Beijing: People's Bank of China.

People's Bank of China (2013). Notice on Issues Related to Investment in the Inter-bank Bond Market by Qualified Foreign Institutional Investors. PBC Document No. 69. Beijing: People's Bank of China.

People's Bank of China (2014). Opinions of the PBC Financial Measures to Support the China (Shanghai) Pilot Free Trade Zone. Beijing: People's Bank of China.

Takagi, Shinji (2011). Internationalizing the Yen, 1984–2003: Unfinished Agenda or Mission Impossible? *BIS Papers*, No. 61, 75–92. Basel: Bank for International Settlements.

The Giovannini Group (2001). Cross-Border Clearing and Settlement Arrangements in the European Union. Brussels: European Commission.

UN COMTRADE Database.

Wignaraja, Ganeshan (2013). Regional Trade Agreements and Enterprises in Southeast Asia. ADBI Working Paper No. 442. Tokyo: Asian Development Bank Institute.

Yu, Yongding (2012). Revisiting the Internationalization of the Yuan. ADBI Working Paper No. 366. Tokyo: Asian Development Bank Institute.

Appendix

Table 7.   Intensity of Intra-industry Trade with ASEAN+3: Grubel and Lloyd Index

		1995	2000	2005	2007	2012	2014
China	Parts and components	0.66	0.54	0.54	0.60	0.63	0.68
	Capital Goods	0.58	0.75	0.67	0.71	0.86	0.96
	Consumer Goods	0.26	0.21	0.37	0.47	0.51	0.44
Japan	Parts and components	0.63	0.78	0.81	0.81	0.84	0.94
	Capital Goods	0.41	0.77	0.89	0.87	0.95	0.93
	Consumer Goods	0.32	0.21	0.29	0.34	0.35	0.19
Korea	Parts and components	0.99	0.95	0.89	0.95	0.81	0.76
	Capital Goods	0.60	0.74	0.92	0.95	0.78	0.97
	Consumer Goods	0.54	0.82	0.79	0.61	0.75	0.64
ASEAN-10	Parts and components	0.85	0.96	0.98	0.99	0.99	0.93
	Capital Goods	0.75	0.85	0.88	0.84	0.76	0.86
	Consumer Goods	0.80	0.87	0.93	0.92	0.93	0.88

Sources: UN COMTRADE Database.

Chapter 3

Issues and Prospects of International Monetary Reforms: East Asian Perspectives

Yung Chul Park

1. Introduction

The international monetary system is such a familiar and extensively used terminology that most people think they know what it is, but in reality there is no widely accepted definition. Different people have different ideas as to what the system refers to. In this chapter we follow the explanation by Truman (2011) that the system is "the set of obligations, rules, conventions, procedures, and institutions that shape the international economic and financial policies of governments in their interactions with each other."

There has been a general consensus among economists and policy makers that international monetary system (IMS) is inefficient and unstable and its failures in the international monetary system are responsible for the global crisis. The IMS exacerbated, rather than helped contain, the severity, contagion, duration, and the resulting social consequences of the 2008 global financial crisis for both advanced and emerging economies. Unless overhauled, there was the fear that some of the failures including lack of an adequate adjustment mechanism, lack of global liquidity, and excessive volatility in exchange rates and capital flows would continue to destabilize global financial markets in the future.

In realization of the need to improve its efficiency and stability, at the time of the 2011 Cannes G20 summit, the French government proposed an agenda for IMS reform, which included surveillance of the global economy and financial system, global financial safety nets, the control of global capital flows, reserve currencies and global liquidity, and IMS governance. In particular, as Farhi *et al.* (2011) point out, the IMS has failed to provide an optimal provision of global liquidity because of a chronic and severe shortage of reserve assets.

The reform of the international monetary system has long been the subject of intense debate, elicited numerous studies, and produced an endless list of reform proposals at many international fora including the G20. Globalization and the growing share of emerging economies in international trade and financial transactions have brought to the fore a number of issues that are not new, but that have yet to be attended to and changed the balance of power in a system that still retains the imprint of the 1944 Bretton Woods Conference.

The financial crisis of 2008 has further laid bare the defects of the current system and underscored the urgency of reform. The G20 has taken up reform issues, but has made little progress, in particular since 2011 it has been preoccupied with other global issues such as the euro-area crisis, and deflation combined with slow growth, putting the IMS reform on the back burner for the past four years.

This chapter reviews some of the ongoing debates on reform from the perspectives of East Asia. Section 2 looks at the deficiencies of the current reserve currency system. Despite all its deficiencies, the US dollar will remain the dominant reserve currency. In a financially integrated global economy, financial linkages and the financing conditions in the main global centers of international finance — the US financial center being the dominant one — govern the conditions in the rest of the world regardless of the exchange rate regime (see Rey 2013).[1]

Once the regularity and predictability of the global financial cycle are established, developed and emerging economies would be subject to a

---

[1] In the finance literature, explaining the global stock market integration, a number of authors search for world factors common to all stock markets that drive the co-movement in stock prices and the presence of a strong group factor, a world factor constructed from country indices by principal components, value-weighting, or some other method of aggregating the indexes (see Blackburn and Chidambaran, 2011).

common risk element, which would in turn result in high correlation of flows of capital market instruments including bonds and equities with one another and negative correlation with a measure of uncertainty and market risk aversion such as the VIX. In such a regime, when capital is freely mobile, capital flows, asset prices, and credit expansion co-move across both developed and emerging economies, limiting the effectiveness of free floating in safeguarding independent monetary policy.

Section 2 also discusses the future prospect of the reserve currency system. Despite the anomaly, the US dollar is expected to command a dominant position as a reserve currency. Special Drawing Rights (SDR) could serve as a reserve currency and asset, but politically it is almost impossible to increase its supply enough to replace or complement the dollar. Other reserve currencies may emerge but it is not clear whether a multi-reserve currency system is viable. It is followed in Section 3 by an examination of the future role of other reserve currencies. The euro will survive the ongoing euro-zone crisis, but play a diminished role, and that the outlook for internationalization of the RMB is promising, but depends largely on the prospects of China's financial liberalization and opening.

Section 4 explores the background and merits of capital controls in a new global financial environment. The IMF position has long oscillated between firm hostility and reluctant acceptance. The position has now changed somewhat (IMF 2012). Refining the instruments, and making them better attuned to present-day markets, may bring further changes to the conventional wisdom.

Section 5 deals with developments in regional monetary arrangements. The 2008 crisis has dimmed much of the earlier hope that the Chiang Mai Initiative Multilateralization (CMIM) would become operational. The European debt crisis has made it clear that deep regional monetary integration is more difficult than was officially recognized.

Section 6 examines the prospect of the spread of swap agreements among central banks. In the aftermath of the 2008 collapse of Lehman Brothers, swaps have been activated on larger scale than before. This section explores whether the use of swaps portends a new form of international monetary cooperation. Concluding remarks are in a final section.

2. Reserve Currency System

2.1. The Demise of the US Dollar?

Many economists and policy makers throughout both advanced and emerging economies find it incongruous that the dominant international currency is under the control of a single country — the United States. The global financial crisis that began in 2008 and the ongoing euro-zone sovereign debt crisis have renewed the call for a new arrangement that will end the dollar's supremacy. The World Bank (2011) predicts that by 2025 the US dollar will be replaced by a multi-currency system made up of the dollar, the euro, and the Chinese renminbi (RMB). In the long run such a system could be established, but in the immediate future, the dollar is nowhere near losing its primary international status for the simple reason that there is no replacement.

The dollar's role as the dominant currency for international trade invoicing and payments is of secondary importance even though it is practical and less risky to deal in your own currency. What matters most is the use of dollars as foreign exchange reserves. These reserves are held mostly in US Treasury bills. The value of dollar currency held outside the US is less than 10 percent of the dollar-denominated official reserves.

At the end of 2014, the dollar's share was about 62 percent of total allocated foreign exchange reserves and is likely to decline. The decline, if it continues, does indeed imply that the dollar would be a minor reserve currency by 2025. It is possible that a growing number of emerging economies may decide to acquire new reserves in other currencies than the dollar, such as the euro, pound, Swiss Franc, and the yen. However, it is difficult to imagine that they will hold a substantial share of their reserves in terms of these currencies. The reason is that unlike the United States, none of the countries issuing these international currencies can supply an adequate amount of interest-paying public debt instruments that are both safe and liquid and that central banks want to invest for their reserve holdings.

The need for safety excludes many euro-area governments. Unless the market is deep enough, emergency sales may resemble fire sales that entail capital losses. The safest euro-denominated instruments are issued by the German government. The market for German debt is not very deep, especially in comparison to US Treasuries. At the end of 2014, marketable US federal debt instruments were a multiple of seven of the corresponding German debt instruments. In the same year, the average daily turnover on these instruments was 20 higher for US bonds than for German bonds. The situation is similar for French debt instruments. The US simply plays in a different league.

2.2. Special Drawing Rights (SDR)

The SDR, created by the IMF in 1969, is not a money, but a right for a central bank to obtain dollars, euros, or other currencies of wide international use. It serves as foreign exchange reserves and is more stable in value than that of its composite currencies. These qualities are the reasons why some developing countries and development advocates have been calling for a massive increase in SDR as an alternative to the dollar (Stiglitz 2010).

Farhi *et al.* (2011) argue for greater use of the Special Drawing Rights and incorporating the currencies of the large and rapidly growing emerging economies including the RMB to facilitate the emergence of a private market for SDRs, and allow the IMF to issue SDR-denominated debt. They believe these changes could help the international monetary system evolve and avoid serious financial crisis by increasing the supply of reserve assets.

Whether SDR can become a principal reserve currency depends on both supply and demand. On the supply side, the total stock is SDR204 billion at the end of 2004. This is a trivial amount. If $150 to $300 billion were issued each year, then the stock of SDR would reach about 50 percent of the non-gold reserve in 10 years. But the question remains whether such a large amount of SDR can be issued.

As a potential claim on some currencies, SDR must be underwritten by the central banks that issue these currencies. New SDRs are effectively new dollars, euros, yen, and other widely traded currencies. But no one knows which currencies will be "drawn" — that is, used — and when. No central bank will ever want to create large amounts of money over which it has no control. The appeal of SDRs, that they are not controlled by any national central bank, is also their fundamental weakness.

2.3. A Multiple Reserve Currency System?

Many economists argue that the creation of a more competitive set of reserve currencies could provide more stability in the IMS — as central banks would have a more diversified set of assets to invest, competition among reserve currency countries might instill discipline in their macro-economic policies. This may prevent or at least mitigate the impact of the periodic financial crises the international monetary system has long endured.

Farhi *et al.* (2011) argue that it can only be a matter of time before the global economy will develop a multipolar reserve currency system. The emergence of this multipolar system will increase the supply of reserve assets, thereby solving the Triffin dilemma.

This reasoning is at least incomplete. As noted earlier, a number of observers including the World Bank (2011) believe that the US dollar will eventually be replaced by a multi-currency system made up of the dollar, the euro, and the RMB — plus perhaps the Indian rupiah. Sachs (2012) argues that it is ideal to have at least three or four reserve currencies and a flexible arrangement among them: dollar, euro, RMB, and yen. Eichengreen (2012) also claims the dollar's days as reserve currency are numbered. As its share of global GDP continues to decrease, the United States' capacity to provide dollar liquidity — safe assets such as Treasury bills backed by its power to tax — will also decline. Global liquidity needs will have to be supplemented by other countries.

The key requirements to be a reserve currency are that it be issued by a country with a large financial market, fully integrated in the global financial system, and that the government issues top-rated public debt instruments. At this stage, neither the RMB nor the rupiah is fully convert-ible, and the Chinese and Indian financial markets are not globally inte-grated. Moreover, for various reasons, the financial credibility of their authorities is limited.

For the sake of argument, suppose that these currencies develop into reserve currencies, creating a multipolar reserve currency system. Would this be a viable alternative regime? The benefit is that competition among the world's major reserve currencies can make the macroeconomic policy in reserve currency countries more disciplined.

Against this merit, there are fears that such a system will be unstable. The idea seems to be that asset holders might be tempted to zap between reserve currencies. Just as depositors can run on banks, individual central banks could trigger runs on a particular reserve currency as soon as they become concerned about safety or just returns, and possibly even for political reasons. Although it is difficult to prejudge stability of the multipolar system, the experience so far with two reserve currencies — the dollar and the euro — does not bear out such fears. It appears that central banks, at least the large ones, behave prudently because they stand to be the first to suffer capital losses from a rapid shift in the currency denomination of their reserves.

3. The Euro, the RMB, and Currencies of Other Emerging Economies

3.1. The Euro

Since its launching in 1999, the euro has emerged as a major international reserve currency, second only to the US dollar in terms of the relative importance. However, more than five years after the euro-area sovereign debt crisis broke out in 2009, the end is nowhere in sight. As a result, the euro has lost much of its luster. Many analysts are even predicting the eventual breakup of the euro. The euro will survive the ongoing crisis, but unless euro-area countries are prepared to move further toward political integration by creating a banking union and a fiscal union, they are likely to suffer from recurrence of financial crisis. But Wyplosz (2012) argues that the architecture of the European Monetary Union is essentially sound and that the ongoing crisis has not proved that the euro has been a failure or spells its disappearance. Indeed, he reaches an optimistic conclusion on the euro's future.

The European Monetary Union has been plagued by two critical flaws. One has been the failure to establish discipline in a loosely structured federal arrangement, and the other is the lack of euro-zone-wide integration of banking regulation and supervision. For the euro to survive, both flaws must be rectified by reducing sovereignty in these areas, but there is the possibility that a continuing deterioration of the economic situation could bring anti-euro politicians to power. So far, European voters see European unity as fundamental, although they appear to be furious or desperate.

European leaders agreed in June 2012 to establish a single supervisor for large banks in the euro zone — a necessary step toward establishing a banking union. They also pledged to agree on euro-zone-wide deposit insurance and resolution of failed banks. If they reach that goal, which is far from guaranteed, then one of the two flaws will have been corrected. On the other hand, dealing with fiscal discipline in a coherent and efficient way seems a long way off. Indeed, there is a history of members ignoring fiscal discipline dating back to the earliest stages of the European Union.

3.2. RMB

China's policy announcements leave little doubt that it is deeply committed to elevating the RMB to being a currency used outside China as a unit of account, a medium of exchange, and a store of value. With China's growing economy and its large share in global trade, the RMB will ultimately acquire an international status commensurate with the country's economic weight and trade scale. However, at present it remains largely a non-convertible currency.

Growth of the international use of the RMB has been impressive. In April 2009, the Chinese government announced a pilot scheme for cross-border trade settlements in RMB. Since then the amount of RMB trade settlement has risen dramatically — to 24.5 percent of China's total trade in 2004, albeit from a very low base of 0.27 percent in 2009. Surges in the RMB use in Asia Pacific have been equally impressive. The share of the RMB in SWIFT (Society for Worldwide Interbank Financial Telecommunication) international payments jumped to 31 percent in January–April 2015 — from 7 percent during the same period in 2012. The RMB globalization index measured by Standard Chartered Bank shows that it shot up to 2,089 in 2014 from the 2010 base year.

The dominant position of China in regional trade is likely to increase the use of the RMB. It has been forging strategic alliances with many Southeast Asian countries by establishing a free trade area (FTA) with

ASEAN. China also concluded an FTA with Korea and Taiwan. Many ASEAN countries have been managing their exchange rates against trade-weighted baskets of currencies, so the weight of the RMB is bound to increase. This increase will in turn entail greater exchange rate stability against the RMB. Even if they do not follow strict basket pegging, markets may expect that the dollar exchange rates of Asian countries will move in the same directions as the RMB/dollar rate. As a result, the bilateral exchange rates of ASEAN, Korean, and Taiwan currencies *vis-à-vis* the RMB are likely to remain within a narrow band. The large free trade area will also become a large *de facto* — not necessarily a formal — RMB bloc (Park and Song 2010).

The estimation results in Table 1 show that the coefficients of the RMB/dollar exchange rate are positive and statistically significant in all sample economies except for Indonesia. A one percentage point change in the RMB/dollar exchange rate leads to changes in the local currency/dollar exchange rates of each economy, excluding Indonesia, ranging from a high of 0.62 percent in Korea to a low of 0.23 percent in the Philippines. It appears that all sample countries in Table 1 except for Indonesia intervene in their local currency/dollar foreign exchange markets to stabilize their real effective exchange rates. In so doing, they keep their currencies moving in a narrow band *vis-à-vis* the RMB.

Both Korea and Taiwan do not adopt basket pegging, but could be classified as a weakly managed floater. The large coefficient therefore suggests the market's expectation that an appreciation (a depreciation) of the RMB against the dollar would, other things being equal, improve (worsen) the two economies' current accounts and hence strengthen (weaken) their currencies.

Over time, RMB internationalization will build up internal, as well as external, market forces that will speed China's financial reform. An open financial system will help elevate the status of the RMB as an international currency. It will also reduce the tensions to manageable proportions and improve China's economic relations with the rest of the world, but China does not appear to be in a hurry to construct such a system.

A larger role for the renminbi would help resolve the disparity between China's great economic strength on the global stage and its heavy reliance on foreign currencies. On one hand, China is the world's largest

Beyond the Dollar and the Euro

Table 1. Effects of Changes in the RMB/USD Exchange Rate on the Exchange Rates of Seven East Asian Economies (Sample Period: January 1, 2005 — November 15, 2014)

Variables	Indonesia (Rupiah/US$)	Korea (Won/US$)	Malaysia (Ringgit/US$)	Philippines (Peso/US$)	Singapore (S$/US$)	Taiwan (NT$/US$)	Thailand (Baht/US$)
$\Delta x(-1)$	−0.015	0.008	−0.015	0.011	−0.064***	0.007	−0.054***
	(−0.783)	(0.407)	(−0.194)	(0.529)	(−3.307)	(0.340)	(−2.791)
$\Delta x(-2)$	−0.033	−0.010	−0.002	0.016	−0.021	0.023	0.095***
	(−1.635)	(−0.513)	(−0.085)	(0.789)	(−1.079)	(1.177)	(4.979)
ΔRMB	0.590***	0.711***	0.809***	0.416***	0.708***	0.050***	0.510***
	(5.631)	(4.801)	(11.704)	(5.804)	(10.915)	(11.019)	(8.918)
Δyen	−0.042**	−0.159***	−0.045***	−0.073***	0.068***	0.008***	0.085***
	(−2.492)	(−6.599)	(−4.070)	(−6.455)	(6.496)	(3.448)	(9.220)
D-W	2.013	2.002	2.019	2.032	2.012	2.015	2.024
R2	0.016	0.027	0.055	0.028	0.067	0.055	0.077

Notes: [1]Figures in parentheses are p-values.
[2]*, **, ***: Statistically significant at the 10%, 5%, 1% level respectively.
Sources: Authors' estimation.

exporting country and holds the largest stock of foreign exchange reserves by far ($2.9 trillion held as of end 2010). On the other hand, China faces a massive currency mismatch because transactions by its government, corporations, and other entities with the rest of the world are almost entirely denominated in foreign currencies, primarily US dollars. With private entities in China not able to directly address the currency mismatch, the task falls to the government. In moving to address such issues, Chinese authorities have undertaken the internationalizing of the renminbi on two fronts: (1) developing an offshore renminbi market and (2) encouraging the use of the renminbi in trade invoicing and settlement. Such initiatives are beginning to have an effect in laying the foundation for the renminbi to take on a more important global role.

3.3. Other Currencies of Emerging Economies

Rapid growth in emerging-market economies has led to enormous wealth creation and substantial accumulation of their net claims on the rest of the world, raising the profile of emerging markets in the international financial system as a result. Developing and emerging countries held two-thirds of the world's $9 trillion official foreign exchange reserves as of late 2010, compared to only 37 percent of reserves held at the end of 2000. Sovereign wealth funds and other pools of capital in developing countries have become a major source of international investment. Between 2010 and 2025, the collective net international investment position of major emerging markets is projected to rise to a surplus of more than $15.2 trillion (in 2009 dollars) under the baseline scenario presented in Global Development Horizons (GDH) 2011, offset by a corresponding deficit in today's advanced economies.

Even though the role of emerging markets in international finance is growing, there is a great disparity between their economic size and their role in the international monetary system. At present, no emerging economy has a currency that is used internationally — that is, one in which official reserves are held, goods and services are invoiced, international claims are denominated, and exchange rates are anchored — to any great extent. Virtually all developing countries are exposed to currency mismatch risk in their international trade and investment and financing transactions. Addressing these disparities in the international monetary system needs urgent attention, in terms of both the management of the system (here, the International Monetary Fund continues to play a leading role) and the understanding of long-term forces shaping the future workings of the system.

Looking further ahead, as emerging economies account for an ever-growing share of the global economy and participate more actively in cross-border trade and finance, one sees that their currencies — particularly the renminbi — will inevitably play a more important role in the international financial system.

4. Capital Controls and Exchange Rate Regimes

A long tradition has called for the use of capital controls, preferably market-friendly, to discourage capital movements that are driven by herd behavior as opposed to economic fundamentals (Eichengreen *et al.* 1995). This section looks at the IMF's acceptance of a place for capital controls; whether control of inflows is enough; the effectiveness, instruments, and scope of capital inflow controls; and the role of the G20 in the capital control debate.

There is a vast literature on capital control in emerging economies, which offers conflicting and sometimes confusing insights. A meta-analysis of 37 empirical studies by Reinhart *et al.* (2011) finds that capital controls on inflows enhance independence of monetary policy, changes the composition of capital flows by reducing short-term flows, and moderate real-exchange-rate pressures, but they do not reduce the volume of net flows. In contrast, however, there is little systematic evidence of effectiveness of controls on outflows.

4.1. IMF Advocacy of Capital Controls

The IMF formally signaled guarded support for the use of capital controls in November 2012 (IMF 2012). This represents a break from its long-standing position that free capital mobility is an objective to be achieved by all countries at the earliest possible moment. It can be seen as a response to the unstable capital flows observed since the early 1980s.

The IMF now considers that emerging economies may be justified in imposing controls on inflows. Still, the IMF considers that monetary, fiscal, and macroprudential policies should always be the first line of defense, resorting to capital controls only in certain circumstances, mainly inflow surges where large and unsustainable exchange rate appreciation is bound to precipitate a currency crisis.

As to the nature of controls, the IMF correctly favors market-based restrictions such as taxes or unremunerated reserve requirements (URR) and special licensing requirements on external borrowing. More drastic measures include outright limits or bans on foreign borrowing. Capital controls may cover all, or differentiate among, different forms and maturities of flows — bond, equity, foreign direct investment, and short-term versus long-term instruments.

Capital flows are known to be pro-cyclical in emerging economies (Kaminsky *et al.* 2005; Shin 2010). This is a key reason for a counter-cyclical use of controls on inflows. In addition, financial disruptions in one country can easily spill into neighboring economies, including even those with strong economic fundamentals and sound financial systems. Indeed, during a cyclical upswing, banks turn to funding sources other than domestic deposits. This includes foreign borrowing to finance spending on nontraded goods such as housing. When the boom eventually turns into a bust, foreign lenders become concerned about credit risk and begin to recall existing loans while refusing new credit. The result is a sudden stop of capital inflows and, worse yet, large capital outflows. Since all foreign financial institutions and other lenders do the same, they end up deepening the contraction. This is a key reason for a counter-cyclical use of controls on inflows.

An important question is whether controlling inflows is enough. As stated in Ostry *et al.* (2011), the IMF considers that controlling inflows also moderates outflows of foreign capital. Obviously, the size of potential capital outflows is given by the existing stock of foreign liabilities. In the absence of such a stock, limiting inflows indeed limits potential outflows. But most emerging economies have large stocks of foreign investments. In addition, domestic residents may well move assets abroad; most Latin American crises of the 1980s were marked by capital flight.

There is some evidence that some capital control measures may not reduce the aggregate volume of inflows, but do succeed in lengthening their maturity. In the cases of Chile and Colombia, De Gregorio *et al.* (2000) and Cardenas and Barrera (1997) show that controls had some success in tilting the composition of inflows toward a less vulnerable liability structures.

Does this imply that the controls slow outflows? Controls may lengthen the maturity of new inflows, but not affect the stock of existing external funds, which is likely to dwarf new inflows. This point is also made by Calvo (2010). In addition, investors exposed to a country risk may hedge by taking short positions, which is equivalent to a capital flow (see Dooley 1996).

All this suggests that to be effective, capital controls should be symmetric: if there is a need for controlling capital inflows, there is also a need to control capital outflows.

4.2. Effectiveness, Instruments, and Scope of Capital Inflow Controls

Neither theory nor empirical evidence has been able to provide definitive answers regarding the effectiveness of various instruments of capital controls in moderating capital inflows — particularly in the context of the re-imposition of controls by countries that already have largely open capital accounts. However, the Korean experience during the 2008 global financial crisis throws some light on the matter.

With the deepening of the crisis in 2008, the global wholesale funding market froze, and international commercial banks refused to rollover their short-term reserve-currency loans to Korean borrowers. This was exacerbated by foreign investors dumping their holdings of equities. The huge capital outflows triggered massive currency depreciation. To stem the tide, Korea offered government guarantees to foreign lenders and withdrew the withholding tax on foreign holdings of domestic bonds, but to no avail (Park 2009). Free floating failed to serve as a first line of defense, because expectations of further depreciation put the exchange rate on an implosive trajectory.

When some signs of recovery from the 2008 liquidity crisis appeared by the end of the first quarter of 2009, large amounts of foreign capital again started flowing into Korea. Concerned about the destabilizing consequences of the inflows, Korea's policy makers imposed three capital inflow control measures: caps on foreign exchange forward positions of domestic banks and branches of foreign banks in October 2010; a withholding tax on interest income (at a 14-percent rate) and on capital gains (20 percent) from foreign investments in domestic bonds in January 2011; and a macroprudential stability levy in August 2011.

The withholding tax started biting two months after imposition and lasted for about five months. During this period, however, much of the effectiveness was offset by a surge in equity inflows (Park 2012).

5. ASEAN+3 and Regional Liquidity Support Arrangements

Regional financial cooperation has been pursued in East Asia on three fronts: (i) regional economic surveillance (under the Economic Review and Policy Dialogue (ERPD) supported by the ASEAN+3 Macroeconomic Regional Office (AMRO)); (ii) regional short-term liquidity support facility (the Chiang Mai Initiative (CMI)); and (iii) local currency bond market development.

5.1. Evolution of the Mutual Liquidity Support System in East Asia

In 1999, in the wake of the 1997–98 Asian financial crisis, the 10 member countries of ASEAN plus China, Japan, and Korea, now collectively known as ASEAN+3, met and agreed to enhance the "self-help support mechanism of East Asia." This marked a watershed in regional economic cooperation and integration.

As a first step towards policy cooperation and coordination in preventing crises, in May 2000 a system of bilateral currency swaps, dubbed the Chiang Mai Initiative, was agreed. It was designed to provide liquidity support to the members suffering from short-run balance of payment

problems. In August 2003, the ASEAN+3 launched the Asian Bond
Markets Development Initiative (ABMI) to develop efficient and liquid
bond markets in the region so that regional savings could be investment in
the region. ABMI would also contribute to reducing risk of maturity and
currency mismatches ("double mismatch").

In March 2010, the CMI was replaced by a multilateral currency swap
agreement — the CMI Multilateralization (CMIM). Initial member con-
tributions were $120 billion for liquidity support. This was doubled to
$240 billion at the group's May 2012 meeting. In May 2012 CMIM
became CMIM Stability Facility (CMIM-SF) to distinguish it from a new
prevention program designed to help members prevent a crisis — the
CMIM Precautionary Line (CMIM-PL).

The progress of the ABMI has been slow, but it has been instrumen-
tal in creating a regional credit guarantee system, and exploring the possibility of constructing a regional clearing and settlement system for
cross-border bond transactions.

5.2. Issues in Regional Arrangements in East Asia

Unlike China and Japan, ASEAN as a single entity and Korea are potential borrowers from CMIM. As relatively small open economies, they
are the main beneficiaries from regional economic stability. They could
serve as mediators between China and Japan on a wide range of issues
on which the two countries cannot agree. Not surprisingly, in the early
2000s there was a general consensus that they should play an active role
in promoting ASEAN+3 as a framework for regional integration in
East Asia.

However, the 2008 global financial crisis has changed this view. It has
prompted calls for a review of exchange rate policies and of the strategy
for regional financial and monetary cooperation within ASEAN+3.
In fact, the 2008 crisis was the first opportunity to test the effectiveness of
the CMIM. The outcome was not reassuring. Although in dire need of
liquidity in 2008, Korea simply did not consider approaching CMIM for
a short-term loan.

In fact, none of the ASEAN+3 members suffering from a liquidity
drought did, because the amount of liquidity that could be drawn was too

small to impress currency speculators. Even that small amount was not available quickly because of the cumbersome drawdown procedure, and if a member wanted more liquidity than allowed automatically, it had to subject itself to IMF conditionality.

The 2008 crisis episode suggests it is highly unlikely that any member would ever approach CMIM for liquidity support. Indeed, Hill and Menon (2012) assert CMIM is unusable because there is no actual fund to draw from, only a series of commitments made by the members which may not be honored.

Because a member that needs an amount of liquidity greater than its quota has to turn to the IMF, it may not have any incentive to borrow from the regional arrangement in the first place. Unless ASEAN+3 is able to establish its own surveillance capacity, which appears to be a daunting task, the IMF linkage will remain. At this stage, there is no prospect that the member countries will be able to agree on a viable mechanism that could replace the role of the IMF.

5.3. CMIM's Viability

In addition to the structural flaws that severely limit its effectiveness as an insurance scheme, there are other impediments that cast doubt on the viability of the CMIM.

First, neither China nor Japan has any overriding interest in promoting regional financial integration through the expansion of CMIM. It is unlikely they will ever draw on the liquidity support system. Rather, they are the lenders. Besides, if another member runs into a liquidity crisis, China or Japan may find it more expedient to provide bilateral support or suggest going to the IMF, as they did to Korea during the 2008 financial crisis.

Second, from the beginning, CMIM has been plagued by the competitive and adversarial relationships between China and Japan — the two countries that should play the role Germany and France have played in European integration. Instead, differences in their regional interests make it difficult for them to cooperate on economic integration in East Asia.

As the second largest and most economically advanced economy in the region, Japan was at the forefront of coalescing regional efforts for economic integration. It was Japan that advocated the creation of an Asian Monetary Fund during the 1997–98 Asian financial crisis. Japan also took the leadership in launching the ABMI. But subsequently, beset by deflation, a strong yen, slow growth, and political instability, Japan has not been able to act as a leader of economic integration in East Asia.

For its part, China has been preoccupied with its global role. China's policy makers may see little benefits from East Asian regional integration. Indeed, an empirical analysis by Park and Song (2010) shows that among the East Asian economies, China is likely to benefit the least from regional monetary integration. Perhaps for this reason, together with the fact that China has become a major trader with significant financial power, it has shown more interest in global than in regional issues.

As Eichengreen (2009) points out, China might not have to participate in or promote regional arrangements to attain greater political and economic influence in the region. All it has to do is "wait." The longer it waits, the stronger its economic position in the region. The huge export market it presents to ASEAN+3 members will induce them to integrate with China. However, in all likelihood China will do more than just wait. Reticent to promote regional integration at the level of ASEAN+3, it will be much more active in deepening its economic relations with ASEAN, which China regards as its natural and rightful sphere of influence with strategic interests.

Third, the euro-zone sovereign debt crisis, which laid bare the structural weaknesses of the euro and the lack of consensus in supporting members under extreme market pressure, has made ASEAN+3 members wary of the merits and viability of regional monetary cooperation in East Asia.

All this suggests that although regional arrangements such as CMIM could be an important component of the global liquidity support system, little is known on how they should be structured and managed to be a reliable source of short-term liquidity. The G20 may address the viability of establishing similar arrangements in other regions. But before endorsing other regional arrangements, the G20 may need to undertake a review of the size and operational details of CMIM, together with its linkage with the IMF, to determine whether it could be an effective regional mechanism.

Now that the EU has decided to construct the European Stability Mechanism (ESM), which can be seen as a sort of European Monetary Fund operated independently of the IMF, new questions will arise about the linkages of these regional institutions with the IMF and how their activities could be coordinated to consolidate and improve the efficiency of the global safety net. The G20 may need to undertake a review of these mechanisms.

CMIM can be re-designed as an integrated crisis prevention (provision of temporary foreign exchange liquidity support) and crisis response (for cases of currency crises requiring strong macroeconomic adjustment policies) mechanism. If a country faces temporary foreign exchange liquidity shortage, such as an unexpected episode of rapid short-term capital outflows, and the country passes the CMIM pre-qualification criteria, then CMIM should provide the liquidity to the country without any IMF link or conditionality up to the full amount of the country's swap quota. Quick access to a sufficient amount of swap line is important to gain market confidence and stabilize the situation — as happened in Korea during the global financial crisis. If the problem persists after using the CMIM swap for six months for example, then it is likely to be a crisis situation, rather than a temporary liquidity shortage, and thus policy adjustments may be required. Removing the IMF link altogether will make it much more attractive for countries to access the CMIM swap.

6. Swaps as a Global Safety Net

When the financial crisis erupted in autumn 2008, there was a flight to safety among investors worldwide as they steered their portfolios to hold more US dollars and US government debt. Goldberg *et al.* (2011) argue that this flight would have had severe adverse consequences for exchange rates, interest rates, and asset markets worldwide in the absence of what they call "an unprecedented level of cooperation and coordination among major central banks," in which the Federal Reserve in December 2007 established central bank reciprocal currency swaps with several foreign central banks to ameliorate the drought of dollar funding stresses overseas. These arrangements expanded as the crisis continued throughout

2008 and they remained in place through the end of 2009, becoming an important part of global policy cooperation. The authors point out that currency swap facilities have become an important part of the central bank toolbox for managing and resolving financial crises.

One of the lessons of the 2008 financial crisis is that financial markets are highly susceptible to market failures. Overreaction — euphoria or excessive pessimism — and herding of market participants can trigger uncontrollable chain reactions, including the sudden reversal of capital inflows that can provoke a liquidity crisis. Fears of liquidity crises have been one of the reasons for emerging economies to self-insure by holding large reserves. Large reserves also alleviate somehow the need for capital controls.

If there were a global central bank that assumed the role of lender of last resort, it would make sure that liquidity in the global economy is adequate and that the prices of globally traded assets are not too volatile. It would see to it that liquidity crises do not occur and also prevent runs on banks — at least the systemically important ones. The IMF defines global liquidity as the sum of GDP-weighted M2 or reserve money for the four reserve currencies — the US dollar, the euro, the Japanese yen, and pound sterling (IMF 2010). (For discussions of global liquidity, see BIS (2011) and IMF (2011).)

6.1. Swaps among Major Central Banks

Since it is highly unlikely that the global economy will ever be ready for a global central bank, a second-best solution is needed. This could be a global liquidity safety net. In addition to its role during a crisis, a global safety net could alleviate the fear of being afflicted by liquidity shortages that Eichengreen (2012) foresees as coming in the near future.

The architects of the postwar international monetary system created the IMF as a global safety net. However, as the 2008 crisis has shown, the IMF cannot deal with a situation where liquidity can vanish extraordinarily quickly. Support must be available in days, sometimes hours. This is impossible if an agreement must first be negotiated with the IMF and then approved by its Board. The IMF's role has also been further undermined by the perception — borne out of direct experience — that it sets unnecessarily harsh, sometimes even intrusive, conditions for its lending.

In recognition of these shortcomings, in March 2009 the IMF created three facilities: Flexible Credit Lines (FCL), Precautionary Credit Lines (PCL), and High-Access Standby Arrangement (HAPA).

Because it is largely designed for liquidity crises, FCL can be disbursed very fast. There is no conditionality attached, but lending requires pre-qualification based on high standards of policy making. Three emerging economies — Colombia, Mexico, and Poland — have qualified (as of March 2013) and many others would if they applied.

PCL, which also requires pre-qualification, concerns countries that do not quite qualify for an FCL. They combine limited conditionality and fast disbursement.

HAPA is available for countries that do not quite meet the PCL criteria. HAPA is an accelerated standard standby arrangement available to pre-qualified countries. Costa Rica, El Salvador, and Guatemala have been approved.

Do these new facilities broaden and strengthen the IMF safety? We argue that they do not.

One problem is the stigma attached to anything that looks like having to borrow from the Fund, which has deterred applications. The stigma is likely to wear off over time, and there could be a collective effort, for example within the G20, to encourage more applications, including from developed countries since they have discovered they are not immune from requiring IMF help.

A more serious problem concerns the amounts available from the IMF. The size of financial markets has grown significantly over the last decade. The need for emergency liquidity has grown in proportion — in fact it has grown more. The possibility for investors to take huge negative positions means that liquidity needs may become near-infinite.

Stigma and near-infinite needs explain why a number of central banks have agreed swap arrangements following the Lehman Brothers failure. In December 2007 the US Federal Reserve (Fed) established six-month reciprocal swap agreements with the European Central Bank

(ECB, $20 billion) and the Swiss National Bank (SNB, $4 billion). During the height of the crisis of 2008, similar swap lines were also established with the Bank of Japan (BOJ, $60 billion), Bank of England (BOE, $40 billion), and Bank of Canada (BOC, $10 billion) in September. Less than a month later the Fed made dollars available to the ECB, SNB, BOJ, and BOE in quantities without pre-specified limits. Subsequently the Fed authorized dollar liquidity swap lines with nine additional central banks including those of four emerging economies — Brazil, Mexico, Singapore, and South Korea.

All of these arrangements terminated on February 1, 2010, but three months later, the swap lines with the five major central banks, the BOC, BOE, ECB, BOJ, and SNB, were reinstated. These swap lines were extended through February 1, 2014. As of April 24, 2013, the ECB was the only central bank that had a total value of swaps with the Fed amounting to $7,551 billion.

Korea's swap arrangement was limited to $30 billion. Soon after, Korea enlarged existing swap arrangements with Japan (to $70 billion) and China (to 360 billion RMB, about $50 billion at the time). Park (2011) argues that the Fed–Bank of Korea swap, although of limited size, stopped the run on the won because it was provided by the *de facto* global lender of last resort. This raises the question whether similar support (in terms of size and availability) provided by the IMF could have been as effective.

These swap lines were set up during an emergency. None of the participants — in particular those from emerging economies — apparently considered applying to the IMF. Stigma was certainly a powerful motive. Indeed, the mere knowledge that, say, Switzerland was asking for IMF support could have triggered a massive, quite possibly fatal, run on its two large banks. It must be the case that the resources of the IMF were deemed too slim for the task.

The fact that these arrangements were put in place quickly and worked efficiently may suggest that there is no need for further reform in this direction. This would ignore that the agreements only concerned advanced countries. As globalization deepens and as emerging economies grow, more and more countries may need to establish swap lines with the providers of international currencies. How could that be organized?

6.2. A Cooperative Arrangement among Major Central Banks

One lesson of the 2008 crisis is that today's providers may be tomorrow's users, and *vice versa*. This means that swap agreements should be understood to work both ways. The swaps should concern currencies that are used in financial systems since the purpose is to sustain short-term borrowing by banks and financial institutions when private lenders suddenly withdraw. For many years to come, the US dollar and the euro — assuming the latter survives — will remain the main currencies, although the pound, the yen, and the Swiss franc play non-negligible roles. This implies that the Fed and the ECB will serve as the *de facto* global lenders of last resort and providers of emergency liquidity, alongside the Bank of England, the Bank of Japan, and the Swiss National Bank. Other central banks will join either because they hold large reserves that they are willing to mobilize, or because their own financial systems may face sudden stops of capital inflows. The list could include the central banks of Canada, Australia, and New Zealand, and, of course, the central banks of emerging economies that are active in international finance.

The swaps could be permanent agreements or activated at the time of an emergency using an agreed template. The key issues are: amounts, maturity, and interest rate. Maturity and interest rates could be similar to those for the IMF's FCL, which these swaps are meant to complement because of the required size. Indeed, in principle, swaps are most effective when they are provided in effectively unlimited amounts because this is what it takes to convince markets that the situation is under control. If the G20 countries were to take the initiative and establish swap agreements among themselves, it would send a clear signal that member countries are prepared to avert any impending liquidity crisis.

On the other hand, unlimited swaps raise serious moral hazard issues. A liquidity backing could reduce discipline in managing macroeconomic policy and in overseeing banks and other financial institutions. Clearly, some guarantee will be required. This brings us back to the IMF's pre-qualification process of the FCL and PCL facilities. This observation suggests that unlimited swap agreements could be associated with these facilities. Pre-qualified countries would have access to a first line of defense, the IMF facilities, in case of external imbalances and to unlimited swaps in case of liquidity withdrawal.

Even modest swaps might be effective because they signal official intentions. However, the Korean case is ambiguous in this regard. The won's depreciation continued after the Fed swap was announced. Then, in November, a rally occurred but fizzled out despite announcement of enlarged swaps with Japan and China. It is not at all clear whether the end of depreciation came because of the swap agreements or because the won became under-valued. In any case, the limited swaps did not produce any immediate effect.

Aizenman and Pasricha (2009) reach conclusions that the effects of the announcements of the Federal Reserve's swap arrangements with the central banks of Brazil, Korea, Mexico, and Singapore were not uniform and ambiguous. The authors find that the credit default swap (CDS) spreads of these countries fell with the announcement of the swap facilities but so did the CDS spreads of other emerging-market countries. In fact, they find that the decline in the spreads of most emerging markets had started even before the central bank swaps were announced. However, exchange rates of the countries with these arrangements, on average, appreciate, whereas the exchange rates of countries without swaps depreciate.

7. Conclusion

At this juncture in the debate on the reform of the international monetary system, few proposals seem appealing and agreeable to both advanced and emerging economies. The dollar's role as the dominant reserve currency has been reinforced as the euro-zone economies struggle to keep the single currency arrangement alive. The idea of elevating the status of SDR has been going nowhere because SDRs are claims on international currencies whose potential suppliers have shown no interest in augmenting its supply.

In the meantime, G20 members have lost much of their interest in the reform of the IMS simply because they cannot agree on what they should and could do. There is a lack of division of labor between the G7 and the G20. The BRICs will continue to meet on and off to advance and articulate their causes, including the creation of a BRICs development bank, but they seldom agree on anything of substance. The leaders of ASEAN+3 will continue to promise a bright future of regional economic integration despite their poor batting record.

The future of the international monetary system will hinge a great deal on the prospects for recovery in the euro zone and the rise of China. If the euro-zone economies emerge with regained competitive strength and China continues to grow, joined by India, the pressure for reform will grow. Euro-zone countries will have to deliver on giving up seats on the IMF Executive Board. As the world's currency arrangement increasingly becomes a three-pillar system consisting of the US, China, and the euro zone, the G20's role in economic management would remain largely symbolic.

On the other hand, if the euro-zone crisis drags on and China finds itself in turmoil as it has been in recent periods, the G20 could emerge as the only international forum where solutions are debated. The G20 could agree on what is to be done but few of its decisions will be enforceable. In this state of confusion and uncertainty the global economy will muddle through without knowing where it is going. It would take a major global crisis for G20 leaders to attempt to restart the reform of the international monetary system.

References

Aizenman, Joshua and Gurnain Kaur Pasricha (2009). Selective Swap Arrangements and the Global Financial Crisis: Analysis and Interpretation. NBER Working Papers 14821. Cambridge, Massachusetts: National Bureau of Economic Research.

BIS (2011). Global Liquidity: Insights from the BIS Statistics. Note for a meeting of the G20 sub-working group on global liquidity management. Basel: Bank of International Settlements, March 25.

Calvo, Guillermo A. (2010). Controls on Cyclical Capital Inflows: Some Skeptical Notes. Paper prepared for the XXXI Latin American Network of Central Banks and Finance Ministries, Inter-American Development Bank, April 22–23.

Calvo, Guillermo A. and Carmen M. Reinhart (2000). When Capital Inflows Come to a Sudden Stop: Consequences and Policy Options. In *Reforming the*

International Monetary and Financial System, edited by P. Kenen and A. Swoboda. Washington, DC: International Monetary Fund.

Cardenas, M. and F. Barrera (1997). On the Effectiveness of Capital Controls: The Experience of Colombia during the 1990s. *Journal of Development Economics*, 54(1): 27–57.

Cho, Yoon Je (2012). International Monetary System Reform and the G20. Paper presented at the Conference on Energy, International System and Sustainable Development, Seoul, September 21.

De Gregorio, J., S. Edwards and R. Valdes (2000). Controls on Capital Inflows: Do They Work? *Journal of Development Economics*, 63(1): 59–83.

De Gregorio, José, Barry Eichengreen, Takatoshi Ito, and Charles Wyplosz (1999). *An Independent and Accountable IMF*, Geneva Report on the World Economy 1. London: Center for Economic Policy Research.

Dooley, Michael (1996). A Survey of Academic Literature on Controls over International Capital Transactions. IMF Staff Papers, 43, 639–87.

Eichengreen, Barry (2009). Lessons of the Crisis for Emerging Markets. ADBI Working Paper 179. Tokyo: Asian Development Bank Institute.

Eichengreen, Barry (2012). Is the Dollar Dominance Coming to an End? White Paper. DWS Global Financial Institute.

Eichengreen, Barry, James Tobin and Charles Wyplosz (1995). Two Cases for Sand in the Wheels of International Finance. *Economic Journal*, 105(428): 162–72.

Farhi, Emmanuel, Pierre-Olivier Gourinchas, and Hélène Rey (2011). *Reforming the International Monetary System. Centre for Economic Policy Research.* London: Center for Economic Policy Research.

Goldberg, Linda S., Craig Kennedy, and Jason Miu (2011). Central Bank Dollar Swap Lines and Overseas Dollar Funding Costs. *Economic Policy Review*, 17(1): 3–20.

Hill, Hall and Jayont Menon (2012). Asia's New Financial Safety Net: Is the Chiang Mai Initiative Designed not to Be Used? *Financial Times*, July 25.

IMF (2010). Global Liquidity Expansion: Effects on "Receiving" Economies and Policy Response Options. *Global Financial Stability Report: Meeting New Challenges to Stability and Building a Safer System*, Chapter 4. Washington, DC: International Monetary Fund.

IMF (2011). Measuring Global Liquidity. Technical note for G20 sub-working group on measuring global liquidity. Washington, DC: International Monetary Fund.

IMF (2012). The Liberalization and Management of Capital Flows: An Institutional View. Washington, DC: International Monetary Fund.

Kaminsky, Graciela L., Carmen M. Reinhart and Carlos A. Vegh (2005). When It Rains, It Pours: Procyclical Capital Flows and Macroeconomic Policies. *NBER Macroeconomics Annual*, edited by Mark Gertler and Kenneth Rogoff. Cambridge, Massachusetts: The MIT Press.

Kenen, Peter B., Jeffrey Shafer, Nigel Wicks and Charles Wyplosz (2004). *International Economic and Financial Cooperation: New Issues, New Actors, New Responses*, Geneva Report on the World Economy 6. London: Center for Economic Policy Research.

Kok Report (2004). *Facing the Challenge: The Lisbon Strategy for Growth and Employment — Report from the High Level Group Chaired by Wim Kok*. Luxembourg: Office for Official Publications of the European Communities.

Mervyn, King (2010). Monetary Policy Developments. Speech at the University of Exeter, January 19.

Ostry, Jonathan D., Atish R. Ghosh, Karl Habermeier Luc Laeven, Marcos Chamon, Mahvash S. Qureshi, and Annamaria Kokenyne (2011). Managing Capital Inflows: What Tools to Use? IMF Staff Discussion Note SDN/11/06. Washington, DC: International Monetary Fund.

Park, Yung Chul (2009). Global Economic Recession and East Asia: How Has Korea Managed the Crisis and What Has Learned. Working Paper 209. Seoul: Institute for Monetary and Economic Research, the Bank of Korea.

Park, Yung Chul (2011). The Role of Macroprudential Policy for Financial Stability in East Asia's Emerging Economies. In *Asian Perspectives on Financial Sector Reforms and Regulation*, edited by Masahiro Kawai and Eswar Prasad. Washington, DC: The Brookings Institution.

Park, Yung Chul (2012). A Macroprudential Approach to Financial Supervision and Monetary Policy in Emerging Economies. *KDI Journal of Economic Policy*, 34(1): 3–27.

Park, Yung Chul and Chi-Young Song (2011). RMB Internationalization: Prospects and Implications for Economic Integration in East Asia. *Asian Economic Papers*, 10(3): 42–72.

Park, Yung Chul and Wyplosz Charles (2012). International Monetary Reform: A Critical Appraisal of Some Proposals. ADBI Working Paper 364. Tokyo: Asian Development Bank Institute.

Sachs, Jeffrey (2012). Governor's Seminar, 45th ADB Annual Meetings, Manila, Philippines: Asian Development Bank.

Shin, Hyun Song and Shin, Kwanho (2010). Procyclicality and Monetary Aggregates. NBER Working Paper 16836. Cambridge, Massachusetts: National Bureau of Economic Research.

Shin, Hyun Song (2010). Procyclicality in Advanced and Emerging Economies. ADBI Distinguished Lecture. Tokyo: Asian Development Bank Institute.

Stiglitz, Joseph E. and Members of a UN Commission of Financial Experts (2010). *The Stiglitz Report: Reforming the International Monetary and Financial Systems in the Wake of the Global Crisis*. New York: The New Press.

Truman, Edwin M. (2011). Three Evolutionary Proposals for Reform of the International Monetary System. Extension of prepared remarks delivered at the Bank of Italy's Conference in Memory of Tommaso Padoa-Schioppa, December 16, 2011. Available at http://www.iie.com/publications/papers/truman12162011.PDF (accessed March 1, 2016).

World Bank (2011). *Global Development Horizons 2011 — Multipolarity: The New Global Economy*. Washington, DC: World Bank.

Wyplosz, Charles (2011). The Dollar is the Worst International Currency, Except for All the Others. Unpublished manuscript.

Wyplosz, Charles (2012). The International Monetary System after the Euro Area Sovereign Debt Crisis. Paper presented at the Conference on Energy, International System and Sustainable Development, Seoul, September 21.

Zhang, Liqing (2012). Performing International Monetary System and Internationalization of RMB: A Chinese Perspective. Paper presented at the Conference on Energy, International System and Sustainable Development, Seoul, September 21.

Chapter 4

The Euro-Area Sovereign Debt and Banking Crises: Perspectives from East Asia

Yung Chul Park

1. Introduction and Overview

The 2008 global financial crisis has unleashed market and political forces setting in motion fundamental changes in the governance structure of European Economic and Monetary Union (EEMU). It brought a financial storm to the continent that turned market sentiment against the prospect of those euro-area economies running large fiscal and current account deficits, particularly Greece, Ireland, and Portugal, shutting them out of external funding markets. This change in market sentiment claimed Greece as the first casualty of a capital account crisis that has rocked the entire euro area for more than five years. Unable to refinance its external debt, Greece approached the EU and the IMF for financial assistance in May 2010.

In response, a joint crisis-resolution mechanism providing financial assistance conditional on macroeconomic adjustments and structural reform for Greece, known as the troika, which involves the EC and the ECB on the European side and the IMF on the other side, was established. The Greek crisis was highly contagious. Seven months later, Ireland, having been cut off from external funding, sought financial assistance from the troika. Approximately a year later, Portugal also turned to the troika for a bailout loan as it also succumbed to a similar capital account crisis.

Through June 2015, the troika has provided €403 billion in financial support. Of this, €240 billion, or more than 42 percent, has been for bailing out Greece. The IMF contribution to all three countries amounts to €106.5 billion, equal to 56 percent of its total lending. Despite this huge financial support and imposition of fiscal austerity, financial restructuring, and supply side reform, the prospect of Portugal hangs in the balance and Greece may have to leave the euro. Only Ireland has been successful in returning to markets and robust growth.

In 1997, when three Asian countries — Indonesia, South Korea, and Thailand — were unable to avert a capital account crisis on their own, they requested stand-by loans from the IMF to halt a run on their banking systems and foreign exchange reserves. The IMF injected $41.5 billion — or approximately $55.3 billion in current dollars — into the three countries as financial and policy support. That is about one-tenth of the troika's financial support for the three euro-area-crisis countries.

As in the case of the troika resolution program, the IMF financial support came with policy conditionality that required a large array of internal and external adjustments, as well as a wide range of drastic structural reforms. The direct costs of the restructuring itself, in addition to the loss of output and jobs, were staggering.[1] In sharp contrast to the three European crisis countries, however, the three Asian countries were able to restore financial stability and robust growth within two years (see Table 1a in appendix).

The purpose of this chapter is to conduct a comparative study analyzing and contrasting the role of the IMF in the Asian experience with its role in managing the sovereign debt and banking crises in Greece, Ireland, and Portugal since 2010. This is done from the perspectives of the three Asian crisis countries and, more broadly, those of East Asia.[2] To this end, the study highlights and compares some of the salient features of the IMF's engagement with the crisis countries in Europe and in Asia with the focus on design, implementation, and consequences of the resolution programs.

---

[1] For Korea, the resolution cost amounted to 16 percent of GDP.
[2] In this study, Asia and East Asia are used interchangeably, and so are Europe and the euro area.

At the outset, it should be noted that this study relies mostly on various reports published by the IMF-Article 4 consultation reports, euro-area regional surveillance, Extended Fund Facility (EFF), Ex Post Assessments (EPA) and other occasional papers. As is expected, these official documents do not answer many of the questions or clarify issues East Asia's former and current policy makers and analysts have raised on the role of the IMF in managing the euro-area crisis.

Some of East Asia's perceptions may therefore be biased or misguided as they may have been formed by inaccurate facts and information, but readers should make no mistake about what this chapter intends to do. It does not intend to assess, but mostly to convey East Asia's views on the euro-area crisis and what the EU and the IMF have done to resolve it. The EU and the IMF may respond to or ignore the perceptions.

East Asia's perceptions of the euro-area crisis are understandably diverse, varying from country to country and even among experts knowledgeable of crisis developments in the euro area. Overall, however, interviews conducted for this study reveal that most East Asian countries are frustrated and anxious about the persistency of the Greek crisis. With no end in sight, the crisis has clouded the prospect of durable growth and stability in East Asia. In collaborating with the EU, they believe, the IMF has once again displayed a susceptibility to undue pressure from major IMF stockholders motivated by their political and regional objectives.

They are most vocal in criticizing the IMF's large financial contribution to the European crisis management. If saving EEMU is as important as it has often claimed, they believe the richest monetary union in the world should have borne the bulk of financial assistance to the three crisis countries. A review of interviews, media reports, and other publications suggests that three issues related to the crises in both regions sum up East Asia's concerns and perspectives on the euro-area crisis.

The first is the nature of the crisis. The crisis in the southern flank of Europe is not so much an isolated episode of a few member states in financial difficulty as it is a crisis of the monetary union as a whole, because the meltdown of any one member could have posed not only a threat to the survival of the euro but also of provoking financial turmoil and uncertainties throughout the global economy. This potential risk may have justified the IMF's decision to work not only with individual crisis countries but also with the monetary union they belong to and provide financial assistance on a scale unprecedented in its history.[3]

At the same time, however, the IMF involvement in the euro-area crisis has raised a number of questions in the minds of East Asia's current and former policy makers and pundits (henceforth East Asians for short) as to whether the IMF has a mandate for supporting regional financial arrangements such as EEMU as well as individual countries in crisis and, if it has, whether it should have also addressed the reform of the monetary union. On their part, EU policy makers have been inching towards creating a deeper economic and political union. To many East Asians, achieving this ultimate goal appears to be illusive. If indeed, monetary union without political union is not a viable arrangement and given the rift among members on political unification, is there any justification for the IMF to remain as a partner to the EU in managing the euro-area crisis to support the EU's quest for deeper political integration? Many interviewees for this study say there is not.

A second issue is the relative effectiveness of the two crisis-resolution programs in Asia and Europe. A comparison of the two suggests that as far as the speed of recovery and the amount of IMF financial assistance are concerned, despite their failings, the IMF-supported programs for the three Asian crisis countries were more effective than similar programs organized by the troika for Greece, Ireland, and Portugal. East Asian analysts are wondering why these European programs have not been as successful in bringing the euro-area crisis to an end.

A third is the relevance to the euro-area crisis of the knowledge the IMF gained from its experience with the Asian crisis. In its post mortem of the Asian crisis, the IMF drew many lessons in particular from some of the policy conditions that were misguided and may have inflicted greater costs and pains on the three countries than otherwise by deepening and lengthening the duration of the crisis. This study attempts to identify what these lessons were and more importantly asks how useful they have been in minimizing damage from the euro-area crisis.

---

[3] Further, the Fund could have hardly ignored the request of the EU, when the union, as a group, constitutes the largest bloc (31.5 percent) of voting rights in the IMF.

A fourth issue is related to the role of the IMF as a member of the troika. As widely reported in the media and even in scholarly publications, the IMF has been criticized for having compromised its independence and credibility in collaborating with the EU by assuming the role of a junior partner. The alleged loss of independence has rekindled the debate on the need to reform governance at the IMF. In order to ascertain the validity of this criticism, this chapter explores the genesis, evolution, and workings of the troika.

A comparative study covering six countries in two different regions runs the risk of comparing non-comparable episodes as they may not share many institutional features and structural characteristics. While there are many structural dissimilarities, there is a key commonality running through all six countries: they all borrowed excessively from abroad, certainly beyond their debt servicing capacity, exposing them to a sudden stop in capital inflows that provoked a capital account crisis.

In East Asia, with the onset of the crisis, Indonesia, Korea, and Thailand were not able to borrow from abroad in any of major reserve currencies. Once the 2008 global financial crisis battered the euro area with financial turmoil and uncertainty, financial markets began separating Greece, Ireland, and Portugal from other euro members by limiting or cutting off their access to external funding.[4]

Section 2 delineates some of the salient features of a crisis that originates in the capital rather than current account. In terms of this framework, this section investigates causes and triggers of the crisis in both Asia and Europe. This section also conducts a comparative analysis of the relative effectiveness of the resolution programs for both the Asian and euro-area-crisis countries.

In a post mortem of the Asian crisis, the IMF (2000) identifies a number of lessons it drew from the experience. Important questions are whether they have been heeded and, if they have, how useful they have been in minimizing the fallout of the euro-area crisis. Section 3 identifies four such lessons.

---

[4] It was as if the three euro-area-crisis countries were using a foreign currency as legal tender without the benefits of lender of last resort — in effect losing monetary and fiscal independence.

This is followed in Section 4 by an investigation of the independence and credibility of the IMF as a global financial institution in light of improper influence on the IMF's crisis management exerted by some of its major stockholders. Here, independence is narrowly defined to refer to autonomy and freedom of IMF staff surveillance and macroeconomic and financial analyses upon which its decisions on crisis lending and management are made. A summary and conclusions are in a final section.

2. Causes, Triggers, and Consequences of the Capital Account Crises

All six countries under review suffered from a capital account crisis, although causes, triggers, and dynamics of the crisis evolution differ from country to country. A capital account crisis is defined as a sequence of disruptive macroeconomic adjustments that starts with large capital inflows, often dominated by short-term foreign loans and portfolio investments, relative to the absorptive capacity of the economy, which is followed by their sudden stop or reversal (Yoshitomi and Ohno 1999; IMF 2003; Park 2006). When this occurs, the economy in question shifts to a bad equilibrium characterized by a liquidity crisis.

A sudden reversal of capital inflows freezes financial markets, causing a drought of external liquidity.[5] The evaporation of liquidity sets off a banking crisis in which contraction of bank credit leads to a collapse of domestic demand and subsequently results in a sharp increase in corporate failures and non-performing loans at banks. The economy is then forced to repay its external debt by running current account surpluses either by exporting more or by curtailing import demand.[6]

---

[5] In countries where households and firms cannot borrow from abroad in their own currencies, liquidity refers to foreign currency liquidity.

[6] In emerging economies, a reversal of capital inflows causes a currency crisis which puts the nominal exchange rate on an implosive trajectory or which, in a fixed exchange rate regime, provokes a run on foreign exchange reserves. A capital account crisis in an emerging economy is a run on foreign exchange reserves or its banking system or both.

2.1. Causes and Triggers: East Asia

In the run-up to the 1997 crisis, all three Asian crisis countries had few of the macroeconomic vulnerabilities associated with a current account crisis. They were known for fiscal prudence, high private saving and investment rates well over 30 percent, and low inflation (see Tables 1b and 1c in appendix). Their exchange rates were misaligned, but not so much as to trigger speculative attack. Their current account deficits pointed to a productive and growing economy, as they reflected an excess of investment over savings.[7]

It is true that the three crisis countries had been plagued by inefficiencies and instability rooted in many structural distortions in their financial and corporate sectors and government control over the foreign exchange market and capital movements. These weaknesses had existed for decades and were not unique to the region. In East Asia they were masked by rapid growth. Foreign creditors knew of their existence, but ignored or discounted them because they were not considered serious enough to impair credit quality as long as growth was rapid. Creditors were prepared to lend as much as domestic banks and corporations were willing to borrow. If there were imprudent borrowers, they were matched by equally imprudent lenders. How then did these countries come under such a virulent speculative attack that was highly contagious and persistent?

Growth in East Asia from 1994 through early 1997 had been fueled by a rapid expansion of private investment, boosted by a torrent of capital inflows induced by large interest rate differentials between home and foreign financial markets in the wake of a partial deregulation of capital account transactions. Having gained access to low-cost foreign credit, banks and other financial institutions acted as if there were no bounds in borrowing, mostly short-term, and lending long-term in both local and foreign currencies to domestic borrowers without proper credit analysis. This incurred the twin mismatches of maturity and currency on their

---

[7]Although their macroeconomic performance had worsened in the mid-1990s, the extent and depth of the 1997–98 crisis could not be attributed to structural weaknesses or a deterioration in economic fundamentals.

balance sheets and exposed them to credit risk. In the mid-1990s, a series of external shocks (the devaluation of the Chinese RMB and the Japanese yen and a sharp decline in semiconductor prices) began slashing export earnings, causing a slowdown in growth, a larger deficit in the current account, and declining asset prices in all three countries.

When they saw a fall in foreign exchange reserve holdings, foreign lenders began to question whether Indonesia, South Korea, and Thailand were immune to financial crises like the ones that had plagued Latin America. In Thailand, speculators were taking increasingly large short positions against the baht, but the Bank of Thailand was not deterred in defending the currency by forward-selling official foreign exchange reserves. By the end of June 1997, almost all of the country's reserves had been depleted in this failed attempt. Thai authorities were then forced to float the baht on July 2, 1997. When this last-ditch effort did not help stabilize financial markets or stop capital outflows, Thailand had to seek financial assistance from the IMF about a month and a half later, triggering an Asia-wide financial crisis.[8] Realizing that Indonesia had similar macro-economic imbalances and structural weaknesses, speculators moved to test the resilience of the rupiah. As it was becoming impossible to contain the growing market pressure for currency depreciation, the rupiah was allowed to float on August 14, 1997. Within days, the currency lost much of its value *vis-à-vis* the US dollar. Banks, which had funded much of their long-term lending to corporations with un-hedged, short-term offshore loans in US dollars, were unable to secure new short-term loans or renew existing ones when the rupiah was on a downward spiral. Indonesia announced its decision to seek financial assistance from the IMF on October 8, 1997.[9]

As to Korea, by September 1997 foreign bank rollover of short-term loans had fallen to alarming levels and the Bank of Korea had lost most of

---

[8] Financial support for Thailand was about $4 billion over a 34-month period. Additional bilateral and multilateral assistance came to $17.2 billion. Thailand drew only $14.1 billion before leaving the Fund program in September 1999.

[9] Total funding included a $10 billion stand-by loan and $8 billion from multilateral and $18 billion from bilateral donors. Because of the delay in implementation of bank and corporate restructuring, the IMF-supported program was suspended in September 1999. A newly elected government negotiated a new three-year extended arrangement for about $5 billion in February 2000.

its reserves. Even then, policy makers continued to intervene in the foreign exchange market as if they had a plenty of ammunition and with the hope of defending the won. Two months later Korea had nearly run out of reserves and had no choice but to approach the IMF for assistance, which it did on November 21, 1997.

On December 3, the IMF announced its rescue package for Korea, consisting of $21 billion from its own resources and $37 billion from other multilateral sources. The IMF would phase in the disbursement of funds conditional on meeting policy reform targets that included 73 structural policy commitments, many in areas not relevant to crisis management. Initially the IMF disbursed $9.1 billion, but the amount was not enough to impress the market. On December 24, $10 billion out of the backup financing was added to the IMF disbursement together with the bail-in of foreign creditors who agreed to lengthen the maturity of their short-term loans.

2.2. Causes and Triggers: Euro Area

At the time of the crisis in 2010, both Greece and Portugal had a relatively small trade sector, but a fully open financial system that grew rapidly after joining the euro. Ironically, trade and financial integration with the rest of Europe sowed the seeds of crisis in both countries.[10]

After accession to the EU (1981 for Greece, 1986 for Portugal) the relative prices of the tradables of the two countries began converging to those of European and global markets (see Estrada, Galí, and López-Salido 2013). The accession did not help Greece and Portugal to diversify their export products, largely because they had small and inefficient manufacturing sectors and growth was hampered by rigidities in their labor and product markets and appreciation of the real exchange rate.[11]

---

[10] Throughout the 1980s and 1990s, both the Greek and Portuguese economies performed very poorly. Between 1990 and 2000, per capital incomes of the two countries grew on average about 1.6 percent per annum, well below the EU average of 2 percent.

[11] In 2012, the top five export products in Portugal were: Refined Petroleum (7.4%), Cars (4.7%), Vehicle Parts (3.7%), Leather Footwear (3.3%), and Uncoated Paper (2.5%). In Greece they were: Refined Petroleum (35%), Packaged Medicaments (3.1%),

It did open a floodgate for imports as import prices fell markedly. These developments raised the relative prices of non-tradables, causing a shift of labor and capital to the non-tradable sector and, as a consequence, a gaping current account deficit, which reached 15 percent of GDP in Greece and more than 10 percent in Portugal in 2008 (see Table 1h in appendix).

Taking advantage of the newly gained access to low-cost funding, both Greece and Portugal borrowed heavily to finance domestic spending. Unlike the Asian three, most of their international loans were not used to finance investment in the tradable sector, but to support their social welfare systems, including financing government spending for wages and generous pension benefits in the public sector, while tax evasion was rampant. Much of the borrowing was for consumption to close the gap in living standards *vis-à-vis* richer euro members.

Foreign creditors were willing to invest in Greek and Portuguese bonds as if they were government bonds issued jointly by all euro-area members. By the end of 2009, the external debt of Greece had reached 254.5 percent of GDP from 136.3 percent four years earlier. Portugal also exploited access to low-cost funding as its borrowing rates fell markedly after joining the EEMU. As in Greece, most foreign loans were channeled to financing government–private sector joint investment in services and network industries, household mortgages, and consumption. Foreign borrowing of Portugal went from 214.3 to 338.2 percent of GDP (See Table 1j in appendix).[12]

With the global financial crisis spiraling out of control, risk-averse investors, frightened by the virulence of the crisis, began retrenching to domestic and safe-haven markets, drastically reducing the volume of cross-border capital flows within Europe and between continents. Beginning in early 2010, dwindling capital flows made Greece and

---

Aluminum Plating (1.9%), Non-fillet Fresh Fish (1.7%), and Raw Cotton (1.7%). See OEC (Observatory of Economic Complexity): https://atlas.media.mit.edu/en/profile/country/prt/.

[12]According to IMF (2013), Greece is perhaps the only member of the euro area where the government plays a leading role in economic development. Reflecting this, government spending rose to more than 54 percent of GDP by 2009. Therefore, it was not surprising that the bulk of foreign debt was concentrated in the public sector.

Portugal highly vulnerable to a reversal of capital inflows, something that soon took place in earnest.

Greece was the first economy in the euro area shut out of the cross-border wholesale funding market. After the Lehman shock in September 2008, spreads on Greek government bonds over 10-year German bunds jumped to 300 bps compared to about 50 bps before the crisis. Standard and Poor's downgraded Greece from A+ to A in January 2009 and so did Fitch from A− to BBB+ in October 2009, when projections of the budget deficit for 2009 and public debt were sharply increased. With this, external liquidity evaporated: Greece fell into a financial crisis towards the end of 2009 that has tormented the euro area ever since.[13]

In May 2010, Greece requested a 3-year Stand-By Arrangement under the exceptional access policy and the emergency financing mechanism for €30 billion or 3,212 percent of quota. Greece could not meet some of the IMF four rules for the Extended Fund Facility (EFF). Of the four rules, the second one stipulating a high probability of public debt sustainability was the criterion IMF staff could not assure the board of its prospect.[14] To ensure Greece's borrowing from the EFF, the staff had to add a new condition to rule 2, where "a high risk of spillover effects provided an alternative justification for exceptional access" when debt was not sustainable with high probability on the ground that "spillovers from Greece would threaten the euro area and the global economy" (IMF 2013, 11) at a time when there was no firewall in the euro area.

In East Asia's view, the rule change allowing the largest financial assistance to a single country in the history of the IMF meant that since every crisis has a risk of contagion, any country vulnerable to financial turmoil could access the EFF and that it opened the door for the IMF to address a crisis in not only in individual countries, but also regional financial arrangements such as EEMU.

If this fear of contagion was what IMF staff was concerned about, the €30 billion together with the EU financial assistance of €80 billion was

---

[13] It was not until May 2010 that the EC, ECB, and the IMF were able to organize a financial assistance package.

[14] The four rules are: (i) exceptional balance of payment pressures; (ii) high probability of public debt sustainability; (iii) good prospect of returning to capital market; and (iv) a strong prospect of the program success.

hardly sufficient to prevent the Greek crisis spilling over into both Ireland and Portugal within a year. This failure raises a serious question on the IMF independence as a member of the troika. If the staff realized a high probability of this failure as it said it had in its 2013 report, many East Asians ask why it did not insist more forcefully on considering an alternative strategy such as debt restructuring.

Between 2005 and 2009, Portugal was running a large deficit — more than 10 percent of GDP annually — and in 2009 fiscal deficit more than doubled, to almost 10 percent of GDP, lifting up sovereign spreads to post-euro record highs. Standard and Poor's, Moody's, and Fitch all downgraded its sovereign ratings. Although Portugal held out as long as it could before turning to the IMF for financial assistance, structural rigidities, large budget deficits (see Table 1f in appendix), and the loss of competitiveness all pointed to vulnerabilities as perilous as for Greece. In the face of growing fiscal and current account deficits, the country had to be bailed out when it requested €26 billion (2,305.7 percent of quota) financial assistance from the IMF under the EFF arrangement, as it could not return to external funding markets. It was a year after Greece approached the IMF for a similar assistance.

Unlike Greece and Portugal, however, Ireland had made great strides in building strong economic fundamentals by espousing an outward development strategy in the process of integrating its economy into the European single market. Its exports rose to more than 100 percent of GDP just before the 2010 crisis. It restructured export industries to specialize in high-value-added products such as information technology, services, and pharmaceuticals. Attracted by this economic success, foreign credit and investment began flooding the Irish economy.

Most of these inflows were intermediated through the banking sector to finance real property development. The subsequent increase in property prices stoked a consumption boom and pushed up wages and consumer prices, generating a large current account deficit amounting to 6 percent of GDP in 2008. Gross external debt as a percentage of GDP jumped up to 892.6 percent in 2009 from less than 540 percent of GDP four years earlier. The real estate bubble burst around 2007. With the increase in non-performing loans and deposit withdrawal, the banking system became dysfunctional and the economy slid into a deep recession in the following year.

The recession was compounded by the global financial crisis of 2008 that locked Irish banks out of global and regional wholesale funding markets. The budget deficit soared to over 30 percent of GDP in 2010 as a result of the economic contraction, falling property prices, and government guarantees for depositors and investors at insolvent banks. The level of public debt as a percentage of GDP more than doubled to 87.4 percent of GDP between 2000 and 2010. Unable to return to external funding markets, Ireland sought IMF assistance amounting to €22.5 billion (2,321.8 percent of quota) under the EFF arrangement, making it the first victim of cross-border contagion from the Greek crisis. At the time of approval, IMF staff assured the board that all four rules for EFF were met.

In retrospect, the euro-area crisis reflects a gross failure of pre-crisis surveillance of the euro area. To many East Asian analysts, an intriguing question is why surveillance of the crisis countries by EU institutions, such as the ECB and core members of the euro area, had for so long been oblivious to the massive accumulation of external borrowing and misallocation of foreign capital in the three crisis countries. They also argue, on its part, the IMF cannot be free from the criticism that its surveillance had also failed to articulate the risk of the growing fiscal and current account imbalances eroding the foundation of stability of the monetary union.

As argued below, in so far as structural defects of the euro architecture were in part responsible for the runaway external borrowing in the three crisis countries, euro-area policy makers had a limited number of options for restraining the growing imbalances. Under these circumstances, perhaps they were hoping that if capital inflows were used to finance productive investment at a lower cost than before, the crisis countries, in particular Greece and Portugal, would be able to grow faster to reduce the imbalances to manageable proportions and help the two countries to catch up with the living standards of core members.

2.3. Flaws in the EEMU Architecture

While economic mismanagement should be blamed mostly for creating a fertile ground for speculation in Greece, Ireland, and Portugal, it is also true that structural flaws in the euro architecture played a significant part in the buildup and propagation of the crisis. The eruption of the US sub-prime crisis in 2007 and the subsequent global financial crisis in 2008 revealed serious cracks in the structure that exposed the entire monetary union to the risk of financial crisis. Nevertheless, euro-area policy makers were unaware of, or ignored, the possibility that members with a large accumulation of internal and external imbalances would fall into a crisis, let alone that, if it did, the crisis would threaten the very viability of the EEMU.

This raises two contentious questions. One is whether the EU and the IMF should have treated explicitly structural reforms of the EEMU as part of the troika programs. Another is whether and how the resolution burden should be shared between crisis and non-crisis or core members of the euro area. It is a political issue, which is not likely to render an easy solution.

Some of the structural flaws of EEMU are:

— Current account imbalances among euro members matter: indeed, they mattered a great deal as a trigger of the crisis in the southern periphery. If a member efficient in managing its economy runs a surplus, it is likely to be matched by deficits in other members of a monetary union.[15] Those deficits may or may not be benign. If the source of deficit is private sector investment over saving, deficit countries are expected to restore current account balance by fiscal tightening and internal deprecation through cutting cost and improving productivity in the tradable sector. If the source is primarily government overspending, austerity may be in order.

The Stability and Growth Pact (SGP) and no bailout clause — the two keystones for intra-regional stability in the euro area — are designed to prevent the emergence of large fiscal and external imbalances among members. The SGP has been repeatedly breached, and the no bailout clause lost its credibility long ago. As long as the current account deficit could be financed with foreign loans, governments were inclined to set aside or defer addressing the underlying

---

[15] See Tresssel *et al.* (2014) for adjustments in euro-area deficit countries.

problems. For this reason, the countries in the southern periphery were prone to running large current account deficits. When deficits are persistent and large, the market's remedy can be brutal: it abruptly stops lending.[16] Since the crisis, the SGP has been reinforced by more stringent rules, but recent debates on fiscal rules in the EU leave uncertain as to whether the six packs, fiscal compact, and two packs will be easily enforced and effective and whether there is any realistic chance of establishing a fiscal union.[17]

— Capital inflows and outflows between members within the union also matter, but there is no mechanism that can tame volatility of capital flows in times of financial market turbulences.

— There was no EU- or euro-area-wide safety net capable of extricating members in crisis or preventing cross-border contagion of financial market turbulences before creating the European Stability Mechanism (ESM), a permanent bailout fund, in 2012.

— The euro area does not have a lender of last resort. Despite what its name may imply, the ECB is not a lender of last resort, although it has various means of supplying liquidity, including emergency liquidity assistance (ELA). However, it should be noted that the ECB's own rules stipulate that it can only provide ELA "to a solvent financial institution, or group of solvent financial institutions, which is facing temporary liquidity problems through national central banks." Since financial supervision and crisis resolution have been nationally organized, the national central banks have provided emergency liquidity assistance to illiquid but solvent banks on approval by the ECB's governing council, which may reject the assistance, if it does not correspond to "objectives and tasks" of the eurosystem. For this reason, national central banks do not have the capacity to supply the liquidity needed to fend off a run on their banking system as a whole or to pay off sovereign debt.

---

[16] For a more extensive discussion see Wyplosz (2014).

[17] See Mody (2014). Wolff (2014) who argues that "the EU must avoid another useless fight over its fiscal rules and instead use political capital to foster growth".

2.4. Recovery and Relative Efficiency of Resolution Programs in Asia and Europe

Weaknesses in financial and corporate sectors were at the heart of the Asian crisis. It was therefore no surprise that bank and corporate restructuring, which was an integral part of external debt resolution, was the main thrust of the IMF-supported programs. These programs were complemented by (i) contractionary monetary policy and a massive devaluation in transition to a free floating regime, and (ii) supply side reforms of trade, the regulatory system (including strengthening competition laws), labor markets, and public enterprises.

In the euro area, all three euro-area-crisis countries were also subjected to shifts to bad equilibria. Except for Ireland, however, the shifts in both Greece and Portugal were propelled by market concern about sustainability of sovereign debts.[18]

The troika program for Ireland reflected much of the IMF's Asian resolution strategy, whereas the bailout schemes for Greece and Portugal were geared to reducing sovereign debts, which called for a greater emphasis on austerity as a means of restoring fiscal and current account balances and supply side reform for efficiency improvements.

Judging by the speed of recovery and financial costs adjusted for the size of the economy, the IMF-supported programs for the three Asian crisis countries, despite their flaws, were more effective in recovering growth and stability and shortening the duration of the crisis than the programs for Greece, Ireland, and Portugal.

As shown in Table 1a, all three Asian countries bounced back in a V-pattern adjustment after 18 months of severe recession.[19] This is mirrored by a sharp deterioration of the sovereign ratings of Korea and Thailand that was followed within a short period by significant upgrades.

---

[18]The self-fulfilling crisis is characterized by the presence of multiple equilibria, see Gros *et al.* (2009) and Wyplosz (2014). As noted by the Fund's evaluation of the Greek crisis (IMF 2013b), debt restructuring in the form of debt rescheduling, interest rate reductions, debt-for-equity swaps, and debt forgiveness might have been a better strategy.

[19]Korea used $19.5 billion from the IMF. It first paid back all loans drawn from other multilateral sources. In August 2001, Korea closed out the $19.5 billion loan from the IMF, 34 months ahead of schedule.

In contrast, the Greek program has been a dismal failure. Ireland exited the troika program in December 2013, followed by Portugal in May 2014, but this does not necessarily mean that they are fully out of the danger zone. Portugal's growth, fueled mostly by consumption spending, has been anemic. This weak growth casts doubt as to sustainability of its sovereign debt.

Ireland, the best performer of the three, has been able to grow faster than any other member of the euro area, reducing its budget deficit and running a current account surplus, but its fiscal deficit as a proportion of GDP is still among the largest in Europe,[20] its national debt remained high at 109.5 percent of GDP at the end of 2014 (see Tables 1f and 1i in appendix), and its banking system, heavily loaded with non-performing loans, remains vulnerable to external shocks such as contagion from a crisis in any other member of the monetary union (see Table 2 in appendix).

In view of these developments, it is too early to judge whether the rescue operations mounted by the EU and the IMF have succeeded in bringing the euro area back on to the path of pre-crisis growth and stability and turned aside the fear of the demise of the euro area. As Wyplosz (2014) puts it, euro-area "policymakers have declared victory prematurely and studiously ignored the risks of a legacy of huge public debts." Sapir, Wolff, Sousa, and Terzi (2014) concur, citing very high unemployment rates and debt levels.

Discussions with East Asian analysts, including those interviewed for this study, provide four possible explanations for the difference in relative performance.

First and foremost, the Asian crisis countries had nowhere to turn for financial assistance other than the IMF. They had to comply with IMF conditionality regardless of whether they believed it was too harsh, too rigid, or too inconsiderate of their economic and political realities.

The interviewees pondered what could have happened if Greece or Portugal were not a member of the EU. They all agreed that if the Asian experience was any guide and the IMF had its own way, it would have been as ruthless as it had been in Asia and brought all three crises in the

---

[20] Only Spain, Slovenia, Portugal, and Cyprus among euro members had higher ratios in 2014.

euro area to an end a long time ago. This does not necessarily mean that the European members of the troika have been softer than the IMF. They have been equally unsparing, but more for the sake of preserving the integrity of EEMU.

A second explanation stresses differences in economic fundamentals. Even a cursory examination of macroeconomic indicators, such as fiscal and current account balances, public debt to GDP, external borrowing as a proportion of GDP, saving and investment rates over 30 percent, and low price inflation (Tables 1b and 1c in appendix), leave little doubt that the Asian three, even including Indonesia, had stronger macroeconomic fundamentals, weighted by the size of the economy, which allowed them to withstand better the vagaries of the crisis compared with their European counterparts.

Third, in Asia the crisis originated in the private sector and the culprits were imprudent banks willing to lend without proper credit risk analysis and to large corporations with an insatiable demand for credit, whereas in Europe, except for Ireland, the main guilty party was none other than the government itself, bent on financing its social welfare system with funds borrowed from abroad rather than tax revenues.

It is likely to be easier to reform the structural weaknesses of the private sector than those of the government sector. In fact, as the Korean experience shows, it is almost impossible to make government carry out its own reform. In Asia, governments had to clean up the wreckages of bankrupt corporations and insolvent financial institutions and to consolidate financial supervision to rein in the banking and corporate sectors. The Asian governments were not blameless, but the public, knowing nowhere to turn to other than the IMF, grudgingly accepted its role as the agent of reform.

In the euro-area crisis, the governments were the targets for restructuring. In Greece, the troika program may have been perceived as an unreasonable demand for dismantling its social welfare system. Even though the system is grossly mismanaged and unsustainable, this perception has persisted in the Greek opposition and exacerbated the stalemate from which Greece and its European creditors have been unable to extricate themselves.

Relatedly, a fourth explanation underscores differences in the mode of adjustment to a crisis. In Asia, a large increase in the current account surplus, much of which was caused by the collapse of investment demand together with a spurt in export earnings induced by massive currency depreciation, turned market sentiment in favor of the three countries, prompting the return of foreign investors and paving the way for a rapid recovery. Such an expenditure switching mechanism was not in operation in Greece or Portugal.

A fifth explanation points to structural defects of the monetary union as impediments to a crisis resolution in the southern periphery. Unless these flaws are rectified, it is difficult to imagine that euro-area policy makers will be able to find a durable solution to ongoing crisis. For example, in the absence of an adjustment mechanism for bilateral current account deficits, the euro area will continue to be vulnerable to asymmetric external shocks among members.

Finally, there was the difference in the external environment. In the late 1990s, trade and global growth was much more favorable to the export-oriented economies of Asia than it has been for Greece, Ireland, and Portugal since 2008. Indeed, if there were no global financial crisis, the fiscal and current account imbalances and structural weaknesses may have never surfaced in the southern periphery.

3. Program Design and Implementation: Asian Crisis Lessons

A review of the IMF-supported programs shows that the causes and unfolding dynamics of the euro-area crisis are similar in many respects to those of the Asian crisis. So are the program designs for macroeconomic adjustments and structural reforms, and the phased-in disbursement of financial assistance conditional on meeting the reform targets. In view of these similarities, it is worthwhile examining whether the troika could have mitigated the adverse impact of economic and political fallout of the euro-zone crisis if it had revisited the knowledge the IMF gained from its experience with the Asian crisis.[21]

---

[21] Pisani-Ferry, Sapir, and Wolff (2013) find that the absence of a clear counterfactual is the most significant challenge for analyzing the troika programs, because financial assistance in the euro area is the first substantial incidence of assistance within a monetary union.

In its post mortem of the Asian crisis, the IMF was specific in drawing lessons from some of its policy conditions that were misguided and may have inflicted greater costs and pains than otherwise (Lane 1999 and IMF 2000). This study attempts to identify what these lessons were and, more importantly, asks how useful they have been in minimizing damage from the euro-area crisis.

3.1. Resolution Strategy: Growth First or Austerity First?

The Greek economy has contracted by a quarter in the five years since the crisis began in 2009, and has seen its sovereign debt soared to 177 percent of GDP at the end of 2014 and unemployment over 25 percent. Many interviewees argue that, more than anything else, the rescue program, with its focus on austerity and structural reform, should bear much of the blame for the dismal state of the Greek economy, a view vigorously challenged by euro-area policy makers (see Schäuble 2015a).

The Asian crisis experience demonstrates that, for heavily indebted countries, the main solution for debt resolution is growth (Park 2001). When the crisis started in 2009, it was obvious that Greece's public debt was not sustainable (IMF 2013), nor was Portugal's. As the IMF's debt sustainability analysis noted (IMF 2011, Annex 1), starting in 2013, Portugal's debt serving capacity would depend on growth. Portugal recorded negative growth in 2013 and from 2014 onward to 2017 is projected to grow by a little over 1 percent.[22] Only Ireland appears to be on

---

In the absence of ECB financing, mostly in the form of ELA, the euro-area crisis could have degenerated into a collapse of the euro-area financial system, which eventually would have risked the breakup of the euro area.

[22] An IMF (2015a) review on Portugal states that the adjustment program has contributed to turning the current account deficit into a surplus, arresting the run-up in private and public debts levels, and restoring full access to sovereign debt markets. But, it goes on to outline a long list of fragilities that could easily reverse what has been achieved. Some of these are associated with apathy to, or delay in, structural reform. Portugal still needs to address a myriad of structural problems including rigid labor markets, high energy prices, a low degree of domestic competition, and a bias in FDI toward non-tradable sectors, if it is to raise growth and absorb the large internal slack. However, fatigue and a sense of complacency about structural reforms may have already taken hold.

its way to a full recovery: it grew 4.8 percent, the fastest in the EU in 2014, and is expected to grow by more than 3 percent for the next two years (see Table 1a in appendix).

At the beginning of the crisis, internal and external imbalances together with deeply entrenched structural frailties of Greece and Portugal were so overwhelming that many Asian interviewees were unanimous in saying that the IMF should have stood firm on debt restructuring as the most realistic resolution strategy. However, even if the eurogroup policy makers agreed to the unsustainability, they could not and would not let them default on or restructure their debts.

Debt default was inconceivable as it could mean exit of both Greece and Portugal from the monetary union and potentially disintegration of the euro area. Debt restructuring had the risk of entailing catastrophic consequences of setting off a massive exodus of creditors from other members, including Spain and Italy, which could also threaten the very existence of the euro area.[23] Even if it did not endanger the viability of the monetary union, other heavily indebted countries might demand similar debt forgiveness. Despite the occasional threat of Greek exit, core members of the euro area were not prepared to force Greece out of the monetary union.

This resolve, however, did not mean that the eurogroup was prepared to do whatever it took to rescue the three countries. In particular, there was no expectation of providing financing sufficient enough to help Greece and Portugal pay down their international debt to a sustainable level, simply because some of the lender countries were not only opposed to financing more than what they had agreed for the troika programs, but also wanted to discipline Greece for its bad behavior.

It was clear by the early 2010 that core members of the euro area were determined to impose austerity and structural reform measures as part of their disciplinary actions against fiscal profligacy on Greece and Portugal. Former US Treasury Secretary Geithner (2014, 442) recalls a meeting of a group of seven finance ministers held in February 2010 where the European ministers were "complaining about Greek profligacy and mendacity. There

---

[23] The eurogroup must also have been concerned about moral hazard. If Greece is allowed to pay off its debt with official sector funding, it may never have incentives to restructure its economy.

were strident calls for austerity and Old Testament justice." Under these circumstances, it appears that eurogroup policy makers had to claim that Greece, Ireland, and Portugal all suffered from a crisis of confidence rooted in structural weaknesses, the remedy for which was to return to markets through austerity and structural reforms.

To judge by the Asian crisis experience, the programs for Greece and Portugal were misguided in that austerity and supply side reform cannot be a substitute for financial assistance in any crisis. It was therefore no surprise that, as in Asia, the programs failed to assuage creditors' fears: they knew that the countries would be hard pressed to pare down government spending and meet the reform conditionality when they were in recession, thereby jeopardizing the successful completion of troika financing.[24]

Practically the entire bailout fund plus some of the primary surplus was used to paying off Greece's international loans. The troika's financial assistance therefore could not release resources for financing domestic investment to enhance growth and stabilizing financial markets.

A growth-first strategy would have been less costly in terms of the actual amount of financing required and in output and employment losses, while easing the constraints on structural reform. Indeed, one of the lessons of the Asian crisis is that an injection of as much financing as needed to support domestic demand to sustain growth while keeping Greece and Portugal on schedule for debt repayment could have reversed, or at least slowed, capital outflows, preventing a collapse of domestic demand and a large increase in the jobless rate, thereby creating a breathing space for an orderly implementation of structural reforms.

This is because if creditors are convinced of a higher probability of repayment of their loans, they are likely to stop withdrawing capital and to be more receptive to a bailing-in by rolling over short-term loans or, better yet, converting them into long-term debt, thereby reducing the actual amount of financial assistance needed to bring a crisis to an end.

The failure of the two Greek programs bears out this argument. By the time the troika stepped in to stop capital outflows in May 2010, the crisis

---

[24] In the Asian crisis, the Fund would have had a better chance of facilitating crisis management if it had made available more financing for bank and corporate restructuring with less stringent monetary policy and structural reform conditions.

might have already impaired the economy so much that the first Greek financial assistance was grossly inadequate to restore market confidence. Not surprisingly, thereafter, Greek economic conditions continued to deteriorate. Greece needed more money to survive the crisis. Greece received a second bailout worth €130 billion with all private creditors holding Greek government bonds required to extend maturities, accept lower interest rates, and a hair-cut of 53.5 percent in face value. In 2012, the eurogroup and Greece had to start negotiations anew for another bailout plan.

Practically all East Asia analysts interviewed argue that the first bailout program had made available a larger amount of financial assistance (say on the order of €250 billion or more) with softer conditions for structural reforms at the outset, it might have had a better chance of averting a further contraction of the Greek economy.

3.2. Failure of Prompt Response

One of the most important lessons of the Asian crisis is that once a capital account crisis strikes, there is little time to lose, given the speed with which capital flows out and currencies depreciate. Foreign creditors sought to be the first out of the door, when they believed that the Asian crisis countries did not have enough money to service their debt. Yet the Asian governments were reluctant to admit they were in a crisis and waited until the last minute before seeking the IMF's assistance. By then their economies had sustained such a severe damage that they required a larger resolution program, with more financial and stringent banking and corporate restructuring, than what they could have negotiated had they approached the IMF earlier.

Having learned the importance of an immediate response, one would expect that IMF staff would have been more aggressive in stressing to the eurogroup the urgency of organizing the preventive measures required to stop capital outflows as soon as possible. In collaborating with its European partners, IMF staff failed to emphasize the importance of immediate responses to symptoms of a crisis when they emerge.

In Asia, it took six weeks from the devaluation of the Thai baht on July 2, 1997 to Thailand's first letter of intent on August 14, which was followed by IMF executive board's approval of the program a week later.

In Indonesia the first letter of intent was signed on October 31 and it was November 5 when the IMF Executive Board approved a three-year stand-by credit of $10.14 billion. Korea decided to approach the IMF on November 19, 1997 and completed negotiations for a stand-by loan about two weeks later. The IMF was not able to act promptly to alleviate fears of foreign lenders and investors in panic simply because policy authorities in the three countries were not able to overcome their perception that being involved with the IMF is a stigma.

If the policy response of the Asian governments and the IMF was slow, euro-area policy makers were moving at a snail's pace. Although by all accounts the crisis started in October 2009, it took more than six months for the EU to organize the troika and the first bailout package for Greece in May 2010. Ireland had slipped into a deep banking crisis that started in 2008, but Irish policy authorities and the troika spent six months after the Greek program was put in place before concluding a rescue program in November 2010. In the case of Portugal, the troika muddled through for a whole year as internal and external balances continued to deteriorate before coming to terms with Portuguese authorities for a bailout loan in April 2011. While the troika was procrastinating, creditors were leaving, deepening the crises further.

It requires some imagination to understand why it took so long for the eurogroup to realize the need for a second program for Greece. Despite the first program, yield spreads against German bund continued to rise and credit rating agencies downgraded Greek bonds to junk status. Finally, more than a year later, on July 21, 2011, against the background of a deepening recession and delayed implementation by the Greek government of the reform conditions, the 17 leaders of euro countries tentatively agreed to a second package.

Actually organizing the second bailout was a slow process. It was more than eight months before all parties ratified the program in March 2012 and rating agencies downgraded Greek bonds to junk status. In contrast, the IMF added $10 billion to Korea's first program just three weeks after it was concluded on December 3, 1997 when the initial package had not stopped outflows of capital and arrested currency depreciation.

Why were euro-area policy makers so slow in coming to grips with the crisis? As Truman (2013) points out, initially they would not accept that Greece was even in crisis. Then they could not agree on what should be done collectively for a timely and effective response. They had no financial or decision-making mechanisms to address the situation and no experience with managing a capital account crisis. Yet they would not allow Greece to go to the IMF despite the fact that they could not agree on among themselves what should be done collectively for a timely and effective response.

Before inviting the IMF to create the troika, the EU had never established either a crisis-funding program or a crisis-resolution mechanism. Nor had it made any institutional arrangement to safeguard against contagion. Only after the crisis broke out did the EU create two temporary mechanisms for crisis funding and resolution — the European Financial Stabilization Mechanism (EFSM), which was allowed to borrow up to a total of €60 billion from financial markets on behalf of the EU, and European Financial Stability Facility (EFSF), which is a special purpose vehicle established for lending to euro-area countries, other than Greece, up to an amount of 440 billion euros, supplemented with a €250 billion IMF commitment.

They had neither enough money nor enough technical expertise to address a crisis as perilous as the Greek meltdown. In October 2012, the two mechanisms were merged to create the European Stability Mechanism as a permanent firewall for the euro area. The ESM has a maximum lending capacity of €750 billion.

Another example of delay regarding Greece was in bailing in creditors. In the Asian crisis, the IMF saw the need of requiring private creditors to maintain their net lending to a debtor country through debt restructuring and controls on capital outflows. However, it was concerned about the downside, as it could exacerbate the contagion that would in the end reduce, rather than increase, private financing (Lane 1999). Nonetheless, the IMF set a precedent for bailing in when, in the midst of a raging crisis, it was able to impose a *de facto* payments standstill in Indonesia and to persuade international lenders to extend maturities of their short-term loans to Korea toward the end of 1997.

In organizing the second Greek program, the troika was able to extract from private creditors a substantial haircut, but until then it had no intention of bailing in private creditors, because many banks from core members had a large exposure to sovereign bonds issued by the crisis countries. These banks did not have enough capital to absorb significant losses in the event of a default or debt restructuring. It is therefore reasonable to argue that the troika was more concerned about driving creditors out of other countries in the euro area where they had substantial exposure if they believed they would be subject to haircuts or maturity extensions of their Greek loans. Such a perception was certain to exacerbate cross-border contagion, thereby threatening collapse of the entire euro-zone banking system.

3.3. Structural Reforms

a. Bank and Corporate Restructuring

By the time the Asian countries approached the IMF, the squeeze on foreign currency liquidity had already wreaked havoc on their economies. Locked out of global debt markets, a large number of ailing financial institutions, including commercial banks with balance sheet mismatches, had to be merged with healthy ones or liquidated. Corporate failures were widespread, as many firms were not able to repay their foreign currency loans or even obtain trade financing. The top priorities of the IMF-supported programs were normalizing bank intermediation and attending to corporate workout to speed up economic recovery.

In organizing the rescue programs in Asia, IMF staff placed bank restructuring and workout of corporate debt at the top of reform priorities, as normalizing bank intermediation was critical to restoring financial stability and reviving growth. The Asian countries liquidated a large number of insolvent banks, merged money-losing but viable banks with healthy ones. They also established state-owned asset management corporations to buy non-performing loans from troubled financial institutions, and to collect those loans. Korea also created a deposit insurance corporation to insure all deposits, including those at non-bank financial institutions, and paid off the depositors at the liquidated institutions, assisted healthy banks to acquire failed financial institutions, and served as the conduit for recapitalization of banks using public funds.

Bank restructuring was costly. For example, by the end of June 2001 when the critical phase was completed, the Korean government had restructured 14 out of 33 commercial banks and 579 non-bank financial institutions — 395 were credit unions — and 13 industrial groups (Chaebol), of which total assets amounted to 7 percent of 2001 GDP, through M&A, liquidation, and revocation of licenses. It spent 137.5 trillion won — 16 percent of 2001 GDP — for restructuring. Of the total, 46 percent (63.5 trillion won) was for recapitalization, 28 percent (38.5 trillion won) for the purchase of non-performing loans, and 22 percent (30.3 trillion won) for deposit insurance.

Except for Ireland which suffered from a banking crisis and the bursting of the real estate bubble, bank and corporate restructuring in Greece and Portugal has not taken priority over other reform measures and hence has not been as extensive as it had been in Asia. The 2013 Ex Post Evaluation (EPE) for Greece states that the banking sector, which was perceived to be relatively sound when the program began, became increasingly vulnerable with the intensification of the recession and the tightening of liquidity. It has no discussion of the state of restructuring of public enterprises or the corporate sector.

As for Portugal, the 2015 first post-program monitoring discussion was concerned about low profitability of the Portuguese banking system, which in turn limited its ability to finance new borrowing for investment as a result of the corporate debt overhang on their balance sheets. It also recommended a more forceful and systemic deleveraging strategy for corporate deleveraging as corporate debt as a percent of GDP started to decline in 2013, but remained well above its pre-crisis level in 2008. The slow pace of bank restructuring has led to a large increase in bad loans at banks. As shown in Table 2, non-performing loans as a share of total loans more than trebled to 33.5 percent in Greece and more than doubled to 10.6 percent in Portugal between 2010 and 2014.

During the Asia crisis, the IMF stepped up its demand for bank and corporate restructuring countries to bring down the non-performing ratio below 5 percent. As shown in Table 2, the ratios fell dramatically in all three countries by transferring bad loans to state-owned asset management companies. An average of similar ratios of high-income economies with GNI per capita $12,736 or more in 2014 was about 4 percent (see Figure 2 in appendix, and World Bank 2015). Judging by this international norm, the shares of bad loans are simply too large, making them highly vulnerable to both internal and external shocks. Instead of removing bad loans, the troika has recapitalized and ECB has provided emergency liquidity assistance to enable banks to continue with intermediation services while keeping a large pile of bad loans on their balance sheets. The Asian experience is that unless such a heavy load of bad loans is alleviated, banks can hardly extend adequate credit to support resumption of domestic demand and economic recovery.

Among the three crisis countries, the banking system restructuring scheme of Ireland has been by far the most extensive in terms of recapitalization and liquidation. The Irish government provided up to €64 billion for recapitalization, about 40 percent of GDP. It closed two of the six large banks, took over a smaller bank, and established a National Asset Management Agency (NAMA) (see Schoenmaker 2015).

While Ireland has been aggressive about bank restructuring, it has been less focused on writing off non-performing loans at banks and hence restructuring debts of ailing corporations. As a result, the share of non-performing loans in total loans more than doubled from 12.5 percent in 2010 to 25.3 percent in 2013. Although non-performing loans were piling up in the aftermath of the bursting of the real property market bubble in 2011 and 2012, Irish banks did not suffer from a lack of liquidity, largely because of the ECB's emergency liquidity assistance, which is not conditional on structural reform.

By August 2011 total liquidity support for the six major Irish banks by the ECB and the Irish Central Bank grew to about €150 billion or 12 percent of their total assets. This liquidity assistance prevented closing of banks, as it allowed them to keep non-performing loans on their balance sheets. However, the large increase in non-performing loans has held back new lending, thereby suppressing domestic demand (see Schoenmaker 2015).[25]

b. Overloading Supply Side Reform

A contentious issue on structural reform raised during the Asian crisis was whether the resolution packages included an overly extensive and

---

[25] Greek banks were able to maintain lending operations with liquidity support from the ECB that had reached almost €90 billion when the support was frozen in June 2015.

complicated list of reform measures that neither creditors nor the general public believed could be carried out on the strict time schedule imposed by the IMF, largely because the governments did not have either the administrative capacity or the will to do so. The same problem has tormented the euro area, more so in Greece and Portugal.

Ireland has been frequently cited by the EU and the IMF as having been the most successful in addressing supply side problems and as an example for other countries that even in severe economic difficulties, structural reforms can offset the negative effects of austerity.

Whelan (2014) argues that this assessment does not correspond to the facts. He shows that, by European standards, markets in Ireland had been deregulated before the crisis, so there were very few structural reforms during the EU–IMF-supported program. In the original EU–IMF-supported program, cutting the minimum wage was the most conspicuous labor market reform. Even this was reversed when a new government renegotiated it in spring 2011.

In Asia, the number of structural policy conditions was very large: at their peak, about 140 in Indonesia, over 90 in Korea, and over 70 in Thailand.[26] If these numbers were excessive, the "laundry lists" for the euro-area crisis countries were simply overwhelming. Sapir, Wolff, Sousa, and Terzi (2014) use the number of pages of the initial troika adjustment program documents as a rough proxy for the extent and details of conditionality. In Greece, the conditionality runs more than 1,800 pages; for Portugal, it is 1,000 pages; and for Ireland it is above 900. Moreover, the number of pages of structural reforms for Greece doubled during the course of the first program. With the second program, it increased another threefold.

The laundry list was not an effective strategy; it backfired for four related reasons in both East Asia and the euro area.

First, many of the reforms were not critical to managing or resolving the financial crisis and restoring macroeconomic stability in the short run,

---

[26] The number of structural policy conditions for Indonesia hit its peak early on and then declined, perhaps reflecting an initial effort to impress the markets with the extent of intended reform and then scaling back as market reaction proved disappointing and as evidence accumulated that implementation capacity or willingness would be lower than anticipated. See Goldstein (2003).

though they may have been essential in improving efficiency of the economy in the long run.

The wide range of reforms could not deliver the needed outcome unless accompanied by careful preparations on prioritization and sequencing. The Asian countries simply did not have the ability to make such preparations and implement so many reforms in so many sectors at the same time. The governments refused to own the reform programs for fear of losing credibility.

The troika faced, but ignored, the same problem. In Greece, the troika disregarded not only the government's limited administrative reform capacity, but also the political constraint imposed by hostility mounted by the groups likely to be adversely affected by reform. Riding on the back of the hostile mood of society, the Greek government has mounted opposition to a proposed structural reform program.[27]

A second reason was that using structural reforms as a substitute for financial assistance undermined the credibility of the rescue packages, the opposite of the intended effect. In the Asian crisis, the IMF sought to impress foreign creditors with a long list of supply side reforms aimed at improving allocative efficiency and export competitiveness. The underlying assumption was that the more effective the structural reform program, the easier it would be to assure foreign creditors of debt repayment and the smaller would be the amount of liquidity support required to bring the crisis to an end.

However, foreign creditors knew all too well that many of the reform measures would take a long time to organize and execute, and this was true even if the countries were determined to put them into effect. Furthermore, it was uncertain whether the reforms would produce the intended results. Foreign creditors were not patient enough to wait for an outcome that was at best uncertain.

---

[27] On April 9 2015, Greek finance minister Yanis Varoufakis said "the word 'reform' [is] a dirty word" (Jolly 2005). If the Greek public doesn't own the overhaul plan, "they will not cooperate, they will see it as a forced occupation." To many, not just Greeks, the harshness of the reforms is perceived as punishment meted out for economic mismanagement and, worse yet, to achieve commercial objectives of major lending countries. The July 5, 2015 referendum demonstrated the point, with over 60% of voters rejecting proposed bailout conditions.

Since the disbursement of IMF loans was conditional on meeting reform targets, foreign creditors wondered whether the crisis countries would have enough money to cover the next repayment of interest and principal. The inference was that the financial assistance the IMF had put together was less than what was needed, and to make up for the shortfall it placed its strategic focus on complementing the programs with a long list of supply side reform. The troika adopted a similar strategy, with similar results.

A third reason was the difficulty of, and conflict of interest in, distributing the costs and benefits of structural reforms in an equitable manner. It was presumed that benefits would outweigh costs in the long run, but the short-run costs were obvious and palpable, borne mostly by those who lost jobs and saw their business fail, whereas it was difficult to determine who would be the ultimate gainers. Since a compromise solution could not be worked out easily, the governments were not able to anchor the reform, vacillating instead between advances and relapses.

Finally, as is well documented on the Asian crisis, structural reform is much more difficult to implement when the economy is in a recession. In theory, supply side reforms boost productivity, output, and employment by shifting workers from low-productivity to productive sectors. When the economy suffers from a collapse of aggregate demand and a rise in business failure, low productivity sectors shed labor, very few of those laid off workers are absorbed by firms in productive sectors that survive the crisis. This is because, in the aftermath of a crisis when future economic prospects are uncertain, domestic demand is shrinking and the cost of credit is high, firms will not expand output. In both Asia and the euro area, structural reform resulted in a high unemployment.

The Asian lesson is that, however critical structural reform is in promoting long-run growth and stability, it cannot restore market confidence in so far as it is carried out at the expense of economic growth in the short run.

3.4. Austerity and the Failure of Expenditure Switching

In managing the Asian crisis, IMF staff, as they had done before with a large number of emerging economies in crisis, laid emphasis on improving the current account balance as the most effective way of restoring investor confidence. This focus dictated tightening fiscal and monetary policy, together with a large currency depreciation or adoption of a flexible exchange rate system, to engineer an expenditure switching policy in which a decrease in domestic demand relative to the supply of output is substituted for a corresponding increase in external demand. Large currency depreciation is critical to the success of the strategy, as it is expected to improve export competitiveness in the short run.

The expenditure switching policy is likely to be more effective in economies with a large trade regime espousing export-led growth.[28]

Both Greece and Portugal are relatively closed economies. Unlike in East Asia, expenditure switching through austerity was not likely to be effective and the IMF knew about it, because their trade sectors were relatively small and the share of manufactures in exports was also small. In contrast, by the time the crisis erupted in 2010, Ireland had cultivated a large trade sector — its export share was one of the highest among euro members — and exported more to non-euro countries.

As noted in Section 3, in Greece, exports consist mostly of agricultural products, fuels, and tourism and shipping receipts. Likewise, Portuguese exports are dominated by agriculture and resource-based low technology products. In all three euro-area-crisis countries, there is limited room for depreciation of the real effective exchange rate through austerity. This is because any depreciation has to come from a fall in prices of tradables and wages. Since 2009, the real effective exchange rates have displayed a downward trend in all three countries (see Figures 1a and 1b in appendix), but because of product and labor market rigidities and a myriad of regulations and other structural impediments, the decline in prices and wages has not been translated into export competitiveness and expansion.

Nonetheless, the IMF country report (2010) produced an extremely rosy forecast of export revenues for Greece growing more than 5 percent annually between 2010 and 2015. Contrary to this optimistic forecast,

---

[28] Initially, this policy did not impress many foreign creditors in the Asian crisis. Only after they saw a large surplus on the current account did market confidence and expectations become better, contributing to capital inflows, although the surplus was initially generated by a deepening recession, not so much by export growth.

tourism receipts — over a third of exports and upwards of 18 percent of GDP — fell with lower demand from high-income countries and increased competition from neighbors whose exchange rates were weakening. Shipping receipts — a third of exports — dropped with lower world trade.

As shown in Table 1g in appendix, Greek exports grew 3.3 percent per year on average between 2010 and 2014; in Portugal, since 2010 export performance has been rather uneven, with years of negative or zero growth and a large expansion in 2013 when exports jumped 12 percent, followed by 4 percent in 2014. However, the increase in export earnings has not been enough to compensate for the decline in domestic demand.

The trade partners of Greece and Portugal are mostly other euro-area members. When the crisis broke out, the two countries were hardly poised to penetrate export markets in Europe. Worse yet, intra-regional trade was shrinking as the continent slid into a severe recession. There was no strong demand for Greek exports or Greek vacations. In contrast, at the time of the crisis in 1997, the Asian countries were benefiting from a favorable trading environment where the booming economies of their major trading partners were ready to absorb their exports.

Ireland endured a crisis distinct from Greece and Portugal, as it was largely a banking crisis driven by panic and overreaction by creditors. Once it was brought under control by bank recapitalization and ECB's ELA, Ireland has been able to resume growth through a substantial expansion of exports. As shown in Figures 1a and 1b in appendix, Ireland had succeeded in improving export competitiveness by cutting down unit labor cost until 2013 when wages stated rising again. The Irish banking crisis has not impaired the efficiency of the tradable sector as much as it might have under different circumstances. Between 2011 and 2014, Irish exports grew on average 6.4 percent per year, the highest among the three euro–area-crisis countries.

4. Collaboration with EU: Independence and Credibility of the IMF

The lack of independence of the IMF has been a matter of concern to the emerging world, as it threatens the effectiveness and credibility of IMF operations and poses the danger of weakening the confidence of the countries it seeks to support. In East Asia's policy circles, the IMF's loss of independence from its major stockholders, who have intervened on many occasions in the formulation and execution of IMF staff's crisis-resolution programs, is not new and is grudgingly accepted as an unavoidable reality. In addressing the euro-area crisis in collaboration with the EU, it may have been placed in a situation where it has been pressured to compromise its independence and credibility.[29]

4.1. The Role of the IMF in the Troika's Crisis Management[30]

Many former and current policy makers, economic analysts, and market participates do not understand the genesis of the EU–IMF collaboration or the troika as the vehicle for crisis management in the euro area. This is largely because relevant information is not readily available. The IMF has yet to explain publicly how it has come to collaborate with the EU and what role it has played as a member of the troika. In the absence of reliable information from the IMF, East Asia's perception of the role has been mostly shaped by media reports of often uncertain reliability. Nevertheless, the following account of the evolution and assessment of the troika operations since 2010 suggests that their critical views and apprehension are not unfounded.

---

[29] Perhaps the most conspicuous case of interference in East Asia is chronicled by Blustein (2001) in his account of the US involvement in the negotiations of reform conditionality for Korea and Indonesia in 1997: the United States dictated the IMF conditionality to include numerous measures such as trade liberalization that were not critical to crisis resolution but were deemed critical to achieving US commercial objectives. Seventeen years later, East Asian interviewees for this study were all disturbed by another exposé by Blustein (2015), where, in managing the euro-area crisis, the IMF may have allowed itself again to compromise its independence in the face of political pressure, this time from its European stockholders. Blustein's account is unconfirmed, but if it is reliable, the IMF was willing to sacrifice its independence for an opportunity to work with euro-area policy makers.

[30] This section is based on author's interviews with officials from the German Ministry of Finance, the ECB, and Bundesbank in Frankfurt and Tokyo, and European and American academics, including staff of research institutes in Brussels, Geneva, Tokyo, and New York.

On the European side, there is a short statement by the heads of state
and the governments of the euro area issued on March 25, 2010 that "as part
of a package involving substantial International Monetary Fund financing
and a majority of European financing, Euro area member states are ready
to contribute to coordinated bilateral loans" (European Council 2010).

On the IMF side, the Staff Report on Request for €30 billion
Stand-By Arrangement for Greece issued in May 2010 (IMF 2010)
emphasizes that coordination with the EC and ECB will be crucial to the
success of the Greek program, but provides no background regarding
EU–IMF collaboration. The report also states that the financial contribution of the IMF and EU will be a constant 3:8 ratio throughout the program period, but does not explain either the criteria for or how the two
institutions arrived at this ratio. A 2014 IMF Factsheet asserts that "Fund
decisions on financing and policy advice are ultimately taken independently of the Troika process by the IMF's 24-member Executive Board"
(IMF 2015b). The statement does not necessarily square with facts.[31]

The East Asian interviewees agree that the IMF could not have sat
by while a serious crisis was building up in Europe, which had systemic
implications for the stability of the global economy. They also realized
that since Greece is a member of the euro area, its collapse raised
the specter of destabilizing the entire European financial sector and,
worse, risking a breakup of the euro area. Under these circumstances,
it was rational for the IMF to seek collaboration with the EU and the
euro area.

Nevertheless, in their view, the IMF, as a global financial institution, should not have entered into an arrangement for collaboration
with the EU on an informal basis. Further, the IMF should not have
accepted or participated in the troika, an ad hoc interim organization,
in the absence of a set of clear rules of governance concerning such
procedural matters as the decision-making process, the authority, and

---

[31] The IMF states that the experience with cooperating with the EC through "the joint
programs in Central and Eastern Europe proved useful." This usefulness was given as the
reason why collaboration was further extended to form a troika when Greece requested
IMF assistance. The Factsheet also claims that the objective of the troika was to ensure
"maximum coherence and efficiency in staff-level program discussions with the three
governments."

accountability of the three members, if only because the troika was slated to make decisions on, among other things, the amount and uses of the IMF resources. These issues were important, because the troika's financial assistance program was the first case of the IMF collaboration with a monetary union.

Few would challenge the rationale behind the EU–IMF rescue program. What troubles the East Asian interviewees is whether the IMF realized that its cooperation with the EU could mean departure from its long-standing standard practice in crisis management, requiring changes in its internal rules of engagement, and, most of all, the modality of collaboration through the troika posed a serious risk of undermining IMF independence and credibility. Even if the IMF had realized the risk, it may have weighed its global role of preventing the spread of the crisis against the possible loss of independence. However, such a benign interpretation has been shattered by Blustein's narrative (2015) on how the IMF came to participate in the troika.

The troika is a structurally flawed institution racked by non-transparency and lack of accountability. For all practical purposes it has been placed under the control by the eurogroup with assistance by the Euro Working Group (EWG). The eurogroup of finance ministers is an informal body in which the president of the ECB, vice president of the EC responsible for Economic and Monetary Affairs and the euro, and the chair of the EWG participate as observers. IMF personnel are sometimes allowed to be present at meetings, but it is not known whether they are allowed to speak.

Although the EC had little technical expertise or experience in working out debt crises, it was put in the driver's seat. The ECB was included, largely because of its liquidity support through the ELA, despite concerns of conflicts of interest arising from imposing conditions on its member governments, from which the bank should remain independent.

An EU report on the workings of the troika (Karas and Hoang-Ngoc 2013) shows that the three partner institutions, each with different mandates and decision-making structures, have an uneven distribution of responsibility and authority, resulting in a lack of appropriate scrutiny and democratic accountability as a whole. The unevenness, which has relegated the IMF to being a junior partner, arose from undue influence exercised by the eurogroup over troika operations.[32]

In working with the EC and the ECB, the IMF has been constrained in asserting its autonomy, mainly because of the eurogroup's implicit assertion that the IMF's authority should be proportional to its financial contribution, which is about one third of the total financial package. Insofar as the eurogroup insists on this proportional rule and "major European creditor countries were not ready to agree on an outright transfer of official sector involvement" (Wolff 2013), the IMF has had no choice but to accept most of the decisions made by the eurogroup.

There has been even a more serious structural problem hampering troika operations. As the largest financial contributor, Germany has taken the helm and dictated most of the group's decisions. Worse yet, it has been unremitting in insisting on austerity. This tenaciousness has become the source of tension and disagreement between the IMF on the one hand and its European partners on the other.

The IMF must have known about the structural flaws of the troika's procedures for interaction and communication, as well as the division of labor among the three members. These flaws have constrained the IMF in being more forceful in arguing for more effective bailout packages that could have mitigated the suffering of the three countries. Until Blustein (2015) came out with his exposé, critics were wondering why the IMF had not been more aggressive in demanding an equal voice or had not threatened to leave the troika. A plausible answer is that, with 56 percent of its lending involved, and knowing the disapproval of its European stockholders, it could not extricate itself.

---

[32]The IMF would ignore any references to having assumed a junior role, but Blustein's interview with Strauss-Kahn shows that the former IMF managing director was so anxious to work with the EU institutions that "he made it clear to EC president José Manuel Durão Barroso that the Fund would accept a sort of junior partner status." He also told Marco Buti, head of economic and monetary affairs, that "We have to be in, but you will be the leader, we will give technical assistance, and some financial resources, but you are leading" (Blustein 2015).

5. Summary and Conclusion

This chapter provides an analysis of the role of the IMF in managing the crises in Greece, Ireland, and Portugal since 2010 from the perspectives of East Asia. Unlike in the 1997 Asian crisis where it was a sole crisis manager, the IMF has been working with the EC and ECB as a member of the troika.

Ireland ended its program in 2013 and Portugal in 2014. Euro-area policy makers may take comfort in believing that, compared to what was expected initially, troika operations have been successful in bringing financial turmoil under control in southern Europe and that, as a member of the troika, the IMF deserves recognition for its contribution.[33] This is too self-serving an assessment. Writing in 2013, Pisani-Ferry, Sapir, and Wolff (2013) were somewhat reticent in assessing the contribution of the troika, noting that the three countries still suffered from severe economic and social hardship.

Since then the Greek crisis has imploded, plunging the entire euro area into a quagmire of blame game that is likely to be hard to escape anytime soon. The EU and Greece are about to negotiate a third bailout plan of which the outcome is anyone's guess. The completion of the troika programs for both Ireland and Portugal can hardly compensate for the anguish and uncertainties the Greek crisis has inflicted on the euro area and the global economy.

Few would deny that the IMF as a global financial institution has responsibility for supporting in some capacity the EU's effort to restore financial stability in the euro area, but it has done so at the risk of incurring a large cost stemming from inefficient use of its financial resources and the loss of reputation. In working with European partners within the troika, from East Asia's perspectives, and in the minds of even non-Asians, the IMF has been constrained in unprecedented ways that have

---

[33] According to German finance minister Wolfgang Schäuble, for instance, "That the European response to the crisis has been ineffective at best, or even counterproductive is simply not accurate. There is strong evidence that Europe is indeed on the right track in addressing the impact, and, most importantly, the causes of the crisis. My diagnosis of the crisis in Europe is that it was first and foremost a crisis of confidence, rooted in structural shortcomings" (Schäuble 2015b).

compromised its credibility and independence. Clearly the IMF was in a difficult position, but even without hindsight one must wonder at some of the IMF's actions.

First, IMF staff were complacent in believing that if a crisis broke out in any euro-area country, EU institutions would be mobilized for crisis resolution. The staff did not believe the euro area was going to ask the IMF for any financial or technical assistance. Beyond that, IMF staff failed to fully appreciate the vulnerabilities of Greece, Ireland, and Portugal to external financial shocks until the 2008 global financial crisis reached the shores of Europe. Nevertheless, when the crisis erupted in Greece, without proper preparations, the IMF accepted eagerly the opportunity to work with the EU.

Second, in joining the troika, the IMF was not attentive to clarifying the terms and conditions for its involvement. As a global institution slated to contribute a large amount of financial assistance, the IMF and the EU should have had a more formal agreement on the operational modality and the role of the IMF in the troika. Instead, the IMF has participated in an ad hoc institution without a clear understanding of the authority, accountability, decision making, or division of labor among the three members. This ambiguity has become one of the sources of tensions between the IMF on the one hand and the European partners on the other.

Third, in managing the euro-area crisis the EU has been much more preoccupied with the risk of financial spillovers of the crises in the three countries into other members such as Spain and Italy and with destabilizing the monetary union than the IMF, which is primarily responsible for preventing the collapse of the three crisis countries.[34] Although the IMF had to change one of the rules for the EFF on the ground of preventing the spillover effects of the crisis, in retrospect the IMF had neither the resources — financial as well as technical — nor the mandate for rescuing a monetary union. This difference in objectives has led to disagreement on a number of issues. Paramount among these were whether the Greek debt should have been restructured sooner and whether senior bondholders of Irish banks should have been bailed in.

---

[34] This point was raised by Pisani-Ferry, Sapir, and Wolff (2013).

Insofar as the EU is determined to accept only those resolution strategies consistent with the objectives of its agenda and more broadly the European project, the IMF may have been constrained to compromise its independence and credibility for the sake of accommodating the EU's demand. However, working within constraints is not the same as compromising principles.

Fourth, some of the core members of the euro area may have felt compelled to discipline the crisis countries for having violated rules and procedures governing EEMU to protect integrity and cohesiveness of the union. Before joining the troika the IMF must have known about the core members' frustration with Greece's irresponsibility and unreliability. After joining the troika, it supported Greek debt relief — making its position public in 2013 — against the wishes of the core members of the euro area bent on punishing Greece.[35]

To the core members, debt relief is a reward for a bad behavior. Therefore, from the beginning there was an irreconcilable difference in the objectives of crisis resolution between the IMF and the eurogroup, because while sympathetic to the core members' discontent, the IMF could not have been party to any strategy designed to discipline other members.

The IMF must have been aware of this potential conflict when it decided to collaborate with the EU yet it has allowed itself to be dragged into internal disputes among the euro-area members from which it has not been able to find an easy way of extricating itself. The IMF has made it clear that it would not participate in the third bailout plan for Greece unless it includes debt restructuring. Many people in East Asia and elsewhere may be wondering why it did not make the same demand when the second bailout was proposed in 2012.

Fifth, some causes of the euro-area crisis originated in structural defects in the architecture of the EEMU. Unless these weaknesses are rectified, there is no guarantee that financial crisis will not recur in the euro area. If the three crisis countries had abided by the SGP and no bailout clause, for instance, by definition they would have never fallen prey to

---

[35] Krugman (2015) goes so far as to suggest that the troika was out to make Greece into an example of what will happen to other debtor countries if they balk at harsh austerity.

crisis. Interviewees for this study could not understand why IMF staff have not been more forceful in demanding structural reform of not only the crisis countries but also the monetary union itself.

If the IMF had faith in moving forward with a deeper political integration as the ultimate solution, it could have insisted on expediting the creation of a banking union and a fiscal union and other reforms under discussion. On the other hand, knowing that how difficult and protracted it would be for the 19 members of the euro area to reach consensus on further political integration, which was certainly beyond the realm of its obligations as a crisis manger, the IMF should have realized the limited room in which it had to operate and should have prepared phasing out its participation in the troika.

Sixth, in crafting resolution strategies, the IMF has failed to implement some of the lessons it learned from its Asian experience. For instance, IMF staff must have known about the risks of austerity, a low priority of banking and corporate reform, and overloading supply side reform, yet it is not clear the extent to which the staff sought to convince its European partners of the importance of the Asian experience.

Finally, there is the question of whether the IMF has been unequal or unbalanced in its approach to managing the crises in both regions as it is often claimed to have demanded a more stringent and inflexible program in Asia than in the euro area. This suspicion arises from IMF's huge financial assistance for the three euro-area-crisis countries and its €250 billion commitment to the ESFS as a firewall in May 2010. To all East Asian interviewees, the IMF financing for Greece, Ireland, and Portugal, which was tantamount to subsidizing wealthy European economies, was as ineffectual as it was unjustifiable and under no circumstances the IMF would have considered contributing as much money to building a firewall in East Asia.

The financial assistance for the three euro-area countries was 2.5 times larger than the support for the Asian three, although the size of the combined GDP of the European three was less than 63 percent of the 1997 Asian total in 2010 US dollars. What was the rationale behind such a large contribution? The euro area did not need IMF's money: as a group of rich countries it certainly had the financial capacity to cover all the resolution financing the troika operations needed.

Was such a large amount needed to contain the spillovers of the crisis in the southern periphery? It was not necessarily so, because in Greece what the IMF thought needed was debt restructuring. Was it for more leverage in decision making at the troika? Given the financing ratio of 3:8 it agreed to, any such voting ratio is immaterial. Regardless of such weights, presumably any two of the troika could outvote the other. Did the Fund then bow to EU's demand?

It is true that as far as the stability of each region and the global economy was concerned, the Asian crisis was not as threatening to global stability as the euro-area crisis has been. Even then much of the Fund's financial support cannot avoid the criticism that it has been mostly wasted and in that sense excessive, because after five years and €240 billion for bailing out Greece, the euro area is yet to see the light at the end of the tunnel.

The interviewees were unanimous in saying that unlike Greece, for example, Asian three did not have any choice but to accept many of the IMF policy conditions and that if the Asian crisis had been promised up front as much IMF financing as the European three were, they would have been spared much of economic and social hardship they suffered during the crisis.

It was clear from the beginning that the eurogroup was not prepared to compromise the objectives or EEMU treaties or, for that matter, relinquish control over the troika. On the part of the IMF, it remains unanswered why the IMF has stayed in the troika. Perhaps, having provided a huge amount of financing and technical expertise, it has not been able to extricate itself from the troika.

Whatever the reasons, Wyplosz (2014) argues that the IMF's joining the troika "was not a felicitous decision." The decision has impaired the IMF's reputation and credibility in the eyes of East Asia's former and current policy makers and many others who have a great deal of influence on shaping IMF's future relations with East Asia.

References

Blustein, Paul (2001). *The Chastening: Inside the Crisis That Rocked the Global Financial System and Humbled the IMF*. New York: Public Affairs.

Blustein, Paul (2015). Laid Low: The IMF, the Euro Zone and the First Rescue of Greece. CIGI Papers No. 61. Center for International Governance Innovation.

Estrada, Ángel, Jordi Galí, and David López-Salido (2013). Patterns of Convergence and Divergence in the Euro Area. *IMF Economic Review*, 61(4): 601–630.

European Council (2010). Statement by the Heads of State and Government of the Euro Area. Available at: http://www.consilium.europa.eu/uedocs/cms_ Data/docs/pressdata/en/ec/113563.pdf (accessed March 31, 2016).

Geithner, Timothy (2014). *Stress Test: Reflections on Financial Crises*. New York: Broadway Books.

Goldstein, Morris (2003). An Evaluation of Proposals to Reform the International Financial Architecture. Cambridge, Massachusetts: National Bureau of Economic Research.

Gros, Daniel, Ulrich Klüh, and Beatrice Weder di Mauro (2009). Reforming global governance: How to make the IMF more independent. Available at: http:// www.voxeu.org/article/reforming-global-governance-how-make-imf-more- independent (accessed October 8, 2015).

IMF (2000). Recovery from the Asian Crisis and the Role of the IMF. IMF Issues Brief, 00/05. Washington, DC: International Monetary Fund.

IMF, Independent Evaluation Office (2003). Evaluation Report — The IMF and Recent Capital Account Crises: Indonesia, Korea, Brazil. Washington, DC: International Monetary Fund.

IMF (2010). Greece: Staff Report on Request for Stand-By Arrangement. *IMF Country Report*, No. 10/110, Article IV Executive Board Consultation. Washington, DC: International Monetary Fund.

IMF (2011). Portugal: Request for a Three-Year Arrangement under the Extended Fund Facility. *IMF Country Report*, No. 11/127. Washington, DC: International Monetary Fund.

IMF (2013). Greece: Ex Post Evaluation of Exceptional Access under the 2010 Stand-By Arrangement. *IMF Country Report*, No. 13/156. Washington, DC: International Monetary Fund.

IMF (2015a). Portugal: First Post-Program Monitoring Discussions-Staff Report; Press Release; and Statement by Executive Director. *IMF Country Report*, No. 15/21. Washington, DC: International Monetary Fund.

IMF (2015b). The IMF and Europe. IMF Factsheet. Available at http://www.imf. org/external/np/exr/facts/europe.htm (accessed April 9, 2015).

Jolly, David (2015). Greek Finance Minister Steers Debt Talk His Way. *The New York Times*, April 9. Available at: http://www.nytimes.com/2015/04/10/business/international/varoufakis-steers-debt-talk-his-way.html (accessed March 31, 2016).

Karas, Othmar and Liem Hoang-Ngoc (2014). On the enquiry on the role and operations of the Troika (ECB, Commission and IMF) with regard to the euro area programme countries. A7-0149/2014. Brussels: Committee on Economic and Monetary Affairs, European Parliament.

Krugman, Paul (2015). Europe's Moment of Truth. *The New York Times* blog, June 27. Available at: http://krugman.blogs.nytimes.com/2015/06/27/europes-moment-of-truth/ (accessed April 1, 2016).

Lane, Timothy (1999). The Asian Financial Crisis: What Have We Learned? *Finance and Development*, 36(3). Washington, DC: International Monetary Fund.

Mody, Ashoka (2014). Are the Eurozone's fiscal rules dying? Bruegel Foundation blog post, October 29. Available at: http://bruegel.org/2014/10/are-the-eurozones-fiscal-rules-dying/ (accessed April 1, 2016).

Park, Yung Chul (2001). The East Asian Dilemma: Restructuring Out or Growing Out? *Essays in International Economics*, No. 223. New Jersey: International Economics Section, Department of Economics, Princeton University.

Park, Yung Chul (2006). *Economic Liberalization and Integration in East Asia*. New York: Oxford University Press.

Pisani-Ferry, Jean, André Sapir, and Guntram Wolff (2013). EU–IMF assistance to euro-area countries: an early assessment. *Bruegel Blueprint Series 19*. Brussels: Bruegel.

Sapir, André, Guntram B. Wolff, Carlos de Sousa, and Alessio Terzi (2014). The Troika and financial assistance in the euro area: successes and failures. Brussels: Committee study on the request of the European Parliament's Economic and Monetary Affairs Committee.

Schäuble, Wolfgang (2015a). Eurozone at a crossroads. Available at: http://www.bundesfinanzministerium.de/Content/EN/Reden/2015/2015-04-17-brookings-washington.html (accessed March 31, 2016).

Schäuble, Wolfgang (2015b). Wolfgang Schäuble on German Priorities and Eurozone Myths. *The New York Times*, April 15. Available at: http://www.nytimes.com/2015/04/16/opinion/wolfgang-schauble-german-priorities-and-eurozone-myths.html?_r=0 (accessed March 31, 2016).

Schoenmaker, Dirk (2015). Stabilizing and Healing the Irish Banking System: Policy Lessons. Dublin: CBI-CEPR-IMF Conference.

Truman, Edwin M. (2013). Asian and European Financial Crises Compared. Working Paper 13-9. Washington, DC: Peterson Institute for International Economics.

Whelan, Karl (2014). Ireland's Economic Crisis: The Good, the Bad and the Ugly. *Journal of Macroeconomics*, 39(Part B): 424–440.

Wolff, Guntram B. (2013). Troika conflict shows need for substantial reform. Bruegel Foundation blog post, June 11. Available at: http://bruegel. org/2013/06/troika-conflict-shows-need-for-substantial-reform/ (accessed April 1, 2016).

Wolff, Guntram B. (2014). Europe needs new investment, not new rules. Bruegel Foundation blog post, June 27. Available at: http://bruegel.org/2014/06/ europe-needs-new-investment-not-new-rules/ (accessed April 1, 2016).

World Bank (2004). *East Asia Update.* East Asia and Pacific Region. Washington, DC: World Bank.

World Bank (2015). World Development Indicators 2015. Washington, DC: World Bank.

Wyplosz, Charles (2014). The Eurozone Crisis: A Near-Perfect Case of Mismanagement. *Economia Marche — Journal of Applied Economics.* Universita' Politecnica delle Marche (I) / Fondazione Aristide Merloni (I), 33(1): 1–13.

Yoshitomi, Masaru and Kenichi Ohno (1999). Capital-Account Crisis and Credit Contraction. ADBI Working Paper No. 2. Tokyo: Asian Development Bank Institute.

Appendix

Table 1. Macroeconomic Indicators of IMF Program Countries in Asia and Europe

a. GDP Growth (Constant Prices)

Europe	2005	2006	2007	2008	2009	2010	2011	2012	2013	2014
Greece	0.9	5.8	3.5	-0.4	-4.4	-5.4	-8.9	-6.6	-3.9	0.8
Ireland	5.7	5.5	4.9	-2.6	-6.4	-0.3	2.8	-0.3	0.2	4.8
Portugal	0.8	1.6	2.5	0.2	-3.0	1.9	-1.8	-4.0	-1.6	0.9
Asia	**1995**	**1996**	**1997**	**1998**	**1999**	**2000**	**2001**	**2002**	**2003**	**2004**
Korea	9.6	7.6	5.9	-5.5	11.3	8.9	4.5	7.4	2.9	4.9
Indonesia	8.2	7.8	4.7	-13.1	0.8	5.0	3.6	4.5	4.8	5.0
Thailand	9.2	5.9	-1.4	-10.5	4.4	4.8	2.2	5.3	7.1	6.3

b. Total Investment (% of GDP)

Europe	2005	2006	2007	2008	2009	2010	2011	2012	2013	2014
Greece	20.87	25.32	26.60	24.72	18.31	16.92	15.80	13.97	11.77	10.58
Ireland	29.40	30.04	28.13	24.02	18.79	15.48	14.98	15.75	15.66	17.39
Portugal	23.66	23.23	23.07	23.57	20.79	21.08	18.60	15.72	14.48	14.88
Asia	**1995**	**1996**	**1997**	**1998**	**1999**	**2000**	**2001**	**2002**	**2003**	**2004**
Korea	39.00	39.68	37.43	27.76	30.92	32.94	31.56	30.94	32.02	32.12
Indonesia	32.40	31.62	32.23	19.23	13.64	25.09	25.32	24.22	28.09	27.36
Thailand	42.09	41.82	33.66	20.45	20.50	22.84	24.10	23.80	24.97	26.79

c. Gross National Saving (% of GDP)

Europe	2005	2006	2007	2008	2009	2010	2011	2012	2013	2014
Greece	13.51	14.50	12.61	10.25	7.42	6.81	5.91	11.49	12.35	11.50
Ireland	25.96	26.49	22.78	18.30	15.74	16.06	15.78	17.32	20.03	23.58
Portugal	12.87	11.92	12.22	10.15	9.04	9.44	10.95	14.13	15.04	15.48
Asia	**1995**	**1996**	**1997**	**1998**	**1999**	**2000**	**2001**	**2002**	**2003**	**2004**
Korea	37.25	35.70	35.58	38.47	35.37	34.80	32.07	31.71	33.76	36.01
Indonesia	23.91	22.99	24.96	17.02	12.49	24.91	24.68	23.36	26.71	24.00
Thailand	34.07	33.77	32.85	33.31	30.66	30.44	28.53	27.49	28.32	28.51

d. Exports of Goods and Services (% of GDP)

Europe	2005	2006	2007	2008	2009	2010	2011	2012	2013	2014
Greece	23.2	23.2	23.8	24.1	19.3	22.2	25.1	27.0	30.2	33.0
Ireland	81.4	79.2	80.4	83.3	90.2	99.8	102.7	107.8	105.8	—
Portugal	27.7	30.9	32.2	32.4	28.0	31.3	35.7	38.7	39.3	39.9
Asia	**1995**	**1996**	**1997**	**1998**	**1999**	**2000**	**2001**	**2002**	**2003**	**2004**
Korea	28.8	27.9	32.4	44.3	37.2	38.6	35.7	33.1	35.4	40.9
Indonesia	26.3	25.8	27.9	53.0	35.5	41.0	39.0	32.7	30.5	32.2
Thailand	41.8	39.3	48.0	58.9	58.3	66.8	65.9	64.2	65.6	70.5

(Continued)

Table 1.   (*Continued*)

e. Imports of Goods and Services (% of GDP)

Europe	2005	2006	2007	2008	2009	2010	2011	2012	2013	2014
Greece	32.5	34.6	37.9	38.6	30.7	31.5	33.1	32.0	33.2	35.3
Ireland	69.7	69.6	71.4	74.3	74.2	81.2	81.1	83.6	82.8	—
Portugal	37.1	39.6	40.2	42.5	35.4	39.0	40.1	39.3	38.3	39.4
Asia	**1995**	**1996**	**1997**	**1998**	**1999**	**2000**	**2001**	**2002**	**2003**	**2004**
Korea	29.9	31.3	33.0	32.1	30.8	35.7	33.5	31.7	33.1	36.7
Indonesia	27.6	26.4	28.1	43.2	27.4	30.5	30.8	26.4	23.1	27.5
Thailand	48.6	45.5	46.6	43.0	45.7	58.1	59.4	57.5	58.8	65.8

f. General Government Net Lending/Borrowing (% of GDP)

Europe	2005	2006	2007	2008	2009	2010	2011	2012	2013	2014
Greece	−5.5	−6.1	−6.7	−9.9	−15.2	−11.1	−10.1	−6.3	−2.8	−2.7
Ireland	1.6	2.8	0.2	−7.0	−13.9	−32.4	−12.6	−8.0	−5.7	−3.9
Portugal	−6.2	−2.0	−3.0	−3.8	−9.8	−11.2	−7.4	−5.6	−4.8	−4.5
Asia	1995	1996	1997	1998	1999	2000	2001	2002	2003	2004
Korea	2.3	2.4	2.4	1.2	1.2	4.2	2.6	3.4	1.6	0.1
Indonesia	0.7	1.1	−1.1	−2.1	−1.1	−1.9	−1.8	−0.6	−1.1	−0.3
Thailand	3.1	2.7	−1.7	−6.3	−9.0	−1.8	−1.8	−6.7	2.1	1.2

g. Volume of Exports of Goods and Services (% Change)

Europe	2005	2006	2007	2008	2009	2010	2011	2012	2013	2014
Greece	3.4	5.2	10.6	3.5	-18.5	4.6	0.0	-0.3	2.8	8.8
Ireland	4.6	5.2	8.8	-0.9	-4.0	6.2	5.5	4.7	1.1	12.6
Portugal	-3.1	9.5	12.3	1.7	-11.7	0.5	9.0	-2.7	11.9	4.0
Asia	**1995**	**1996**	**1997**	**1998**	**1999**	**2000**	**2001**	**2002**	**2003**	**2004**
Korea	27.9	4.1	7.4	-4.8	8.7	12.2	-11.9	7.3	17.0	27.5
Indonesia	12.6	9.9	2.3	-17.3	-1.7	30.8	-7.7	2.1	11.2	14.5
Thailand	22.6	1.6	1.4	-9.5	8.2	13.7	-7.4	6.8	14.0	19.7

Note: Asian data is based on the value of current US dollar.

h. Current Account Balance (% of GDP)

Europe	2005	2006	2007	2008	2009	2010	2011	2012	2013	2014
Greece	-7.4	-10.8	-14.0	-14.5	-10.9	-10.1	-9.9	-2.5	0.6	0.9
Ireland	-3.4	-3.6	-5.4	-5.7	-3.0	0.6	0.8	1.6	4.4	6.2
Portugal	-9.9	-10.7	-9.7	-12.1	-10.4	-10.2	-6.0	-2.1	1.4	0.6
Asia	**1995**	**1996**	**1997**	**1998**	**1999**	**2000**	**2001**	**2002**	**2003**	**2004**
Korea	-1.8	-4.0	-1.8	10.7	4.5	1.9	0.5	0.8	1.7	3.9
Indonesia	-2.8	-2.7	-1.5	3.5	3.4	4.5	4.0	3.7	3.2	1.9
Thailand	-8.1	-8.1	-2.0	12.7	10.1	7.6	4.4	3.7	3.3	1.7

(Continued)

Table 1. (*Continued*)

i. General Government Debt (% of GDP)

Europe	2005	2006	2007	2008	2009	2010	2011	2012	2013	2014
Greece	98.1	102.9	102.8	108.8	126.2	145.7	171.0	156.5	174.9	177.2
Ireland	26.2	23.8	24.0	42.6	62.2	87.4	111.1	121.7	123.3	109.5
Portugal	60.8	61.6	68.4	71.7	83.6	96.2	111.1	125.8	129.7	130.2

Asia	1995	1996	1997	1998	1999	2000	2001	2002	2003	2004
Korea	8.9	8.2	10.2	14.7	16.7	17.1	17.7	17.6	20.4	23.3
Indonesia	—	—	—	—	—	87.4	73.7	62.3	55.6	51.3
Thailand	—	15.2	40.5	49.9	56.6	57.8	57.5	55.1	50.7	49.5

j. Gross External Debt (% of GDP)

Europe	2005	2006	2007	2008	2009	2010	2011	2012	2013	2014
Greece	136.3	158.2	203.6	216.5 (73.6)	254.8 (84.6)	245.3 (102.4)	230.1 (98.8)	299.1 (122.0)	316.1 (130.6)	136.3 (131.8)
Ireland	539.0	641.7	771.2	827.0	892.6	762.1	703.3	667.6	647.5	486.3
Portugal	214.3 (50.0)	252.7 (56.6)	297.6 (64.7)	293.4 (74.6)	338.2 (82.9)	315.4 (81.2)	291.5 (84.7)	318.5 (101.1)	320.8 (99.6)	214.3 (102.8)

Asia	1995	1996	1997	1998	1999	2000	2001	2002	2003	2004
Korea	19.5	24.0	28.8	40.3	28.7	24.1	21.8	21.1	20.3	19.4
Indonesia	61.5	56.7	63.2	158.7	108.4	87.1	82.5	65.5	57.0	53.5
Thailand	59.5	62.0	72.7	93.8	79.0	65.0	58.2	49.6	41.0	36.2

Notes: (1) Net external debt is the value in the parenthesis. (2) Gross External Debt of Ireland excludes the component of "other sectors" due to the IFSC.
Sources: IMF, BIS, EUROSTAT.

Table 2. Nonperforming Loans (NPLs) in the Commercial Banking System of the Crisis-Affected Countries (% of Total Loans)

Asia	1997 Dec	1998 Dec	1999 Dec	2000 Dec	2001 Dec	2002 Dec	2003 Dec
Indonesia[1]	—	—	64.0	57.1	48.8	31.1	18.1
(Excl. IBRA)	7.2	48.6	32.9	18.8	12.1	7.5	6.8
South Korea	8.0	17.2	23.2	14.0	7.4	4.1	4.4
(Excl. KAMCO&KDIC)[2]	6.0	7.3	13.6	8.8	3.3	2.4	2.7
Thailand	—	45.0	41.5	29.7	29.6	34.2	30.6
(Excl.AMCs)	—	45.0	39.9	19.5	11.5	18.1	13.9
Europe	**2010**	**2011**	**2012**	**2013**	**2014**		
Greece	9.1	14.4	23.3	31.9	33.5		
Ireland	12.5	16.1	24.6	25.3	—		
Portugal	5.2	7.5	9.8	10.6	10.8		

Notes: [1] Only includes Indonesian Bank Restructuring Agency (IBRA)'s Asset Management Company.
[2] Korea Asset Management Company (KAMCO) and Korea Deposit Insurance Corp. (KDIC).
Sources: World Bank (2004b) and (2015).

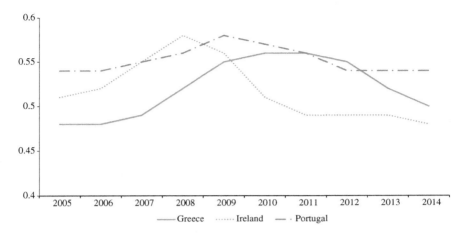

Figure 1a.   Unit Labor Cost (Based on Hours Worked)

Source: ECB.

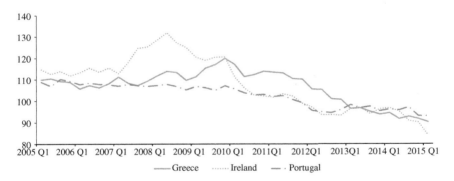

Figure 1b.   Harmonised Competitiveness Indicator Based on Unit Labor Costs (1999 Q1 = 100)

Source: ECB.

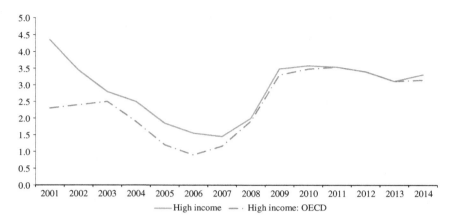

Figure 2.   Bank NPL/Total Gross Loans (%)

Source: World Bank.
* High-income economies are those in which 2014 GNI per capita was $12,736 or more.

Chapter 5

Shaping the Future of the IMS: Regionalization of Selected Asian Currencies*

Il Houng Lee

1. Introduction: A Need to Create an Asian Monetary System

Debates regarding the weakness of the international monetary system (IMS) have often surfaced following financial stresses in the global economy. The latest episode took place in the aftermath of the 2008 global financial crisis; it questioned the desirability of the current IMS that relies heavily on the US dollar (USD). The debate was particularly acute as the financial crisis originated from the United States, traditionally a reliable economy and the issuer of the currency the rest of the world uses to settle a large portion of cross-border transactions and holds as a store of value.

The convenience of using the USD comes with a price tag. Under the current IMS, US monetary conditions are imposed on every other country even if it does not necessarily share cyclical shocks. Choi and Lee (2010), for example, found a significant pass-through of the global monetary policy stance (mainly the US) on 20 Asian countries from 1980 to 2008. Moreover, to the extent that emerging markets (EMs) fix the value of

*An earlier version of this chapter has also been published in the *China Quarterly of International Strategic Studies*, 1(3): 347–372. "Shaping the Future of the IMS: Regionalization of Selected Asian Currencies," Il Houng Lee, *China Quarterly of International Strategic Studies* © 2015 World Century Publishing Corporation and Shanghai Institutes for International Studies.

their currency to the USD — often an optimal policy response from individual country's perspective — the IMS has facilitated bouts of global imbalances. It also exposes countries with non-convertible currencies to foreign exchange crisis risks in times of USD market tightening, such was the case during the 2008 crisis.

For the United States, it is a mixed blessing. On the positive side, it has benefited from a sizable seigniorage. Demand for the USD as a "store of value" and for "precautionary motive" surged during the 2000s as shown in Figure 1, partly in response to the Asian financial crisis, creating a huge base for actual and potential seigniorage. On the negative side, the increase in international reserves under fixed exchange rates by emerging economies, as noted above, exposed the US to reverse spillover of its own policies. US expansionary monetary policy contributed to growing current account deficit and thus capital outflows (Figure 2), which in turn was invested in US assets by surplus countries, facilitating global imbalance.

Too much focus on the global imbalance tends to exert peer pressure on countries to target a certain level of current account balance that may not be optimal from a long-term equilibrium point of view when taking into account each individual country's aging profile. For example, an

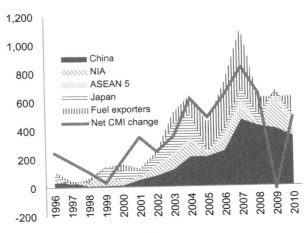

Figure 1.   International Reserves and US Credit Market Instruments (In Billion USD)

Sources: World Economic Outlook, IMF and Flow of Fund, US Federal Reserve (2010).

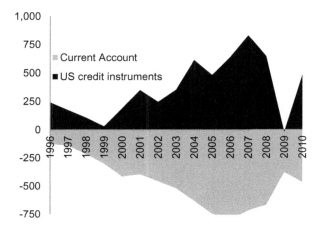

Figure 2. US Current Account Balance and Credit Market Instrument (In Billion USD)

Sources: World Economic Outlook, IMF and Flow of Fund, US Federal Reserve (2010).

analysis by Lee (2015) based on demography alone shows that the United States should have had a current account surplus during most of the 2000s and a deficit during the 2010s while China should have had a current account deficit and a surplus during these two periods, respectively. The gap between the actual and the optimal long-term equilibrium arises either from inadequate level of savings or from investment or both (Lee and Yang 2014).

In fact, an expanded and updated calculation that includes all countries based on the UN's medium growth forecast scenario[1] (Figure 3) shows that China's current account surplus should last somewhat longer while the rest of the world should be the main counterpart of this surplus, not the United States. This is due to the population dynamics, where population in non-advanced plus some emerging economies is expected to increase over the next few decades. For South Korea, it should peak during 2015–2020. A properly functioning IMS should help to ensure the relative balances, reflecting long-term fundamentals.

---

[1] Calculation by the author is based on the "Medium Growth" scenario by the Population Division of the United Nations Department of Economic and Social Affairs of the United Nations Secretariat, 2013, *http://esa.un.org/wpp/* and World Population Prospects: The 2012 Revision, DVD Edition.

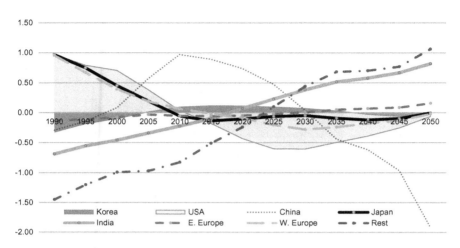

Figure 3. Current Account Adjusted for Multilateral Consistency (In Percentage of World GDP)

Sources: Author's calculation.

Against this background, this chapter proposes an alternative framework which would require governments in selected countries to be more proactive in setting up the necessary institutional structure. More specifically, it proposes a currency arrangement among Asian economies, e.g., ASEAN+3, involving an agreement to settle their current account transactions in any of the selected local currencies. This could be the RMB, the Japanese yen, and a few others including, but not limited to, the Korean won and the Singapore dollar. Since the yen is already a convertible currency and the RMB has already made notable progress toward becoming an international currency, other countries will have to follow some of the steps that China has taken to make their currencies regionally accepted mediums of exchange. This process could be described as "regionalization" and not so much "internationalization" of selected Asian currencies.

If the market responds positively, such an arrangement will lead to a tri-polar and two-tier international monetary system. As a "medium of exchange" and "unit of account," the IMS will be polarized around the USD, the euro, and the RMB, along with few other less-used global reserve currencies. The regionalized currencies will also be used but largely be limited to specific regions and loosely anchored on any of the three main currencies. The second tier, representing international currency demand for "store of value," will be an asymmetric bi-polar system where the USD will dominate, followed by the euro accounting for a smaller share. Gradually, the two tiers will merge as the demand for the RMB deepens with the changing global economic landscape.

Section 2 reviews the recent literature on the factors underlying demand for a reserve currency, usually interpreted as a key measure of a currency's status of internationalization. In Section 3, the above-noted IMS is explained, together with steps that need to be taken for those countries that would like to regionalize their currency. Lessons will be drawn from China's experience. In the final section, incentives and risks for individual countries are discussed.

2. Demand for a Reserve Currency

Recent studies on the demand for reserve currency have focused on the euro and the RMB largely because they are the last ones to join the league of major currencies. History attests to the fact that it takes a long time for any currency to rise as a widely used global reserve currency. Barry Eichengreen (1998), for example, presents historical and econometric evidence to support this finding. He argues in particular that the euro will come to rival the USD as a reserve currency only gradually due to inertia, or the natural advantage of the incumbent (the so-called network externalities). Studies on the RMB also found network externalities, along with the size of the economy, as key determinants shaping the demand for a reserve currency.

2.1. RMB as a Candidate for Reserve Currency

Using panel data, Chen, Peng, and Shu (2009) estimate determinants of demand for reserve currency and find the size of the economy, market development, and network externalities to be the most important factors. On the basis of this study, a counterfactual exercise (using the approach developed primarily by Chinn and Frankel — see Chinn and Frankel

2005) was conducted to investigate the potential share of the RMB as a reserve currency assuming full convertibility. They find the RMB share in the world's total reserves to be 10 percent and 3 percent according to their linear and non-linear models, respectively. This places the RMB at a comparable level with the Japanese yen and British sterling as of 2009 once full convertibility is introduced.

In a similar vein, Wu, Pan, and Zhu (2014) perform a counterfactual simulation for the RMB as a potential international currency, also using the Chinn and Frankel (2005) approach. Based on empirical evidences derived from the performance of the eight major reserve currencies (US dollar, euro, pound sterling, Deutsche mark, French francs, Japanese yen, Swiss franc, and Netherlands guilder) over the past 45 years, they find the size of the economy and network externalities to be the two most significant variables. Exchange rate volatility, understandably, has a negative impact. On this basis, they argue that basic conditions for RMB internationalization are already partly met in that China is the second largest economy and the real RMB exchange rate has been appreciating for the last 20 years, ensuring its relative value is not eroded. In addition, higher real interest rate further induced the demand for the RMB.

Similarly, Huo, Wang, and Shu (2014) use the USD, the British sterling, the Japanese yen, and the euro (Deutsche mark and franc before the euro) during 1980–2012 and find, as shown in Table 1, the size of the economy and the financial market (as measured by the total turnover in the stock market) to be the most important factors in the demand for reserve currency. The result is broadly similar to the findings of Wu, Pan, and Zhu (2014) to the extent that network externalities can be assured if a currency has adequate liquidity in the global market. The coefficient of inflation is significantly negative, which suggests that poor currency stability reduces the possibility of a currency becoming an international reserve currency.

2.2. A Long-term Process

On the basis of these empirical studies, despite the shortcomings of the current IMS, the USD is likely to remain as the main reserve currency for the foreseeable future. Ultimately, it will depend on the market, namely on the confidence that the currency can be converted into goods and services at minimum cost and at short notice. The former requires that

Table 1. Demand for Reserve Currency

Variable	Model 1	Model 2	Model 3[1]	Model 4[2]
Currency-issuing country's GDP to global GDP (lag 1 period)	0.7179*** (0.113)	0.689*** (0.116)	0.638*** (0.132)	0.592*** (0.134)
Inflation	−0.003** (0.002)	—	−0.004** (0.002)	—
Exchange rate	0.001** (0.000)	—	0.001** (0.000)	—
Standard deviation of monthly effective exchange rate	−0.001 (0.002)	−0.000 (0.002)	−0.001 (0.002)	−0.001 (0.002)
Stock turnover to GDP (lag 1 period)	0.019*** (0.005)		0.048*** (0.014)	0.044*** (0.013)
Gold reserves per capita	0.936** (0.370)	0.820** (0.386)	−0.277 (0.538)	−0.427 (0.560)

Notes: [1]With dummy for all variables for 1999.
[2]With dummy for all except for exchange rate and inflation for 1999.
[3]"**" and "***" represent significant levels at 5% and 10% respectively.
Sources: Huo, Wang, and Shu (2014).

the governance that underpins the credibility of the government of the currency-issuing country is sound and sustainable. This is equivalent to "superpower" in Mundell's argument (Mundell 1997) where he notes that "the currency of a superpower would always play a central role in the international monetary system," while the latter would require the currency to have a deep and liquid market, and be supported by a financial infrastructure that enables easy conversion (e.g., clearing, storage, and settlement system), i.e., network externalities. Moreover, the value of the currency has to be stable relative to the price of goods and services, i.e., the inflation rate of the currency-issuing country has to be durably low.

Given the expected shift in the global economic landscape, no one will doubt that the RMB will become a meaningful global reserve currency at some point. Yet it will be a gradual process. An index measuring internationalization of currencies[2] compiled by a People's Bank of China

---

[2]The index is composed of various measures including the share of settlement in global trade, the size of bank credit, international bonds and bills, the amount of global foreign direct investment, and global foreign exchange reserves.

Table 2. Reasons Underlying the Demand for Reserve Currency

	Official Use	Private Use
Medium of exchange	Vehicle currency for foreign exchange intervention	Invoicing trade and financial transaction
Store of value	International reserves	Currency substitution
Unit of account	Anchor for pegging local currency	Denominating trade and financial transaction

Sources: Kenen (1983).

(PBC) study group in 2006 indeed assigns the RMB only a level of 2, in comparison with the USD at 100, followed by the euro at 40 and the Japanese yen close to 30 (People's Bank of China Study Group, 2006). Yet, the demand for the RMB has started to pick up rapidly after the Chinese authorities introduced an institutional framework for settling trade in the RMB and offshore centers for direct exchange of the RMB with other currencies. This demand was underpinned by the strong growth of the Chinese economy and the future landscape of the world order.

To be more precise, the internationalization of a currency can be defined by the type of demand a currency is sought for. As summarized by Kenen (1983) (see Table 2), international demand for the currency should not be different from the three classical functions of money, namely, medium of exchange, store of value, and unit of account.

In China, authorities' efforts have ensured that the first step of internationalization of the RMB is taking place, i.e., as a unit of account and medium of exchange. As long as the institutional framework is in place and full convertibility of the RMB is assured, the market will decide how soon it wants to use the RMB as a store of value. Other Asian countries, except for Japan, have yet to take the first step for regionalization of their currencies, although some of them already have full or almost full convertibility.

Non-economic factors such as military and political influence are often equally important in global affairs. The political system matters as it is key to the governance structure of any monetary system. The actual shift from one reserve currency to another could take place rather rapidly if triggered by global events such as war or major economic shocks

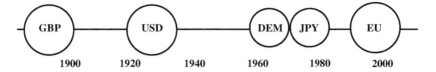

Figure 4. History of Reserve Currency Dominance

Sources: Lee and Yang (2014).

(see Figure 4). For example, the replacement of the pound by the dollar as the world's reserve currency took place relatively fast with the rise of the United States before World War II as the world's dominant political superpower, building on its economic size that overtook the UK about four decades earlier.

The current global political and economic prospects suggest that the market confidence in the US dollar will not likely wane anytime soon. The United States will remain as the dominant military and economic power over the next few decades; demand for US assets and their attractiveness as the most sought after "store of value" across the globe will remain strong. Moreover, the dollar has a deep market with ample liquidity that provides convenience to traders, i.e., network externalities.

3. Possible Shape of the New IMS

3.1. Time for a Change to the IMS

All this notwithstanding, the supremacy of the USD as the main global reserve currency is certainly being challenged. The 2008 global financial crisis, unconventional monetary policy, and the normalization that has yet to take place all undermine market confidence in the US financial market. Moreover, the large public/private debt still needs to be addressed, and the difficult fiscal outlook over the next decade or two exacerbates the uncertainty of whether the value of the dollar can be maintained over the long run. In parallel, the emergence of China as an economic power is affecting the currency landscape in Asia and beyond. For example, the RMB has already established a first trading center outside Asia, in London. The total

Table 3. Global Foreign Exchange Market Turnover (% of Average Daily Turnover of Each Year)

	1989	1992	1995	1998	2001	2004	2007	2010	2013
US dollar	90.0	82.0	83.0	86.8	89.8	88.0	85.6	84.8	87.0
Euro	—	—	—	—	38.0	37.4	37.0	39.0	33.4
Deutsche mark	27.0	40.0	37.0	30.0	—	—	—	—	—
ECU and other EMU currencies	4.0	12.0	15.0	17.0	—	—	—	—	—
Japanese yen	27.0	23.0	24.0	21.8	23.6	20.8	17.2	19.0	23.0
Pound sterling	15.0	14.0	10.0	11.0	13.0	16.4	14.8	12.8	11.8
Chinese yuan	0.0	0.0	0.0	0.0	0.0	0.1	0.5	0.9	2.2
Other currencies	37.0	29.0	31.0	33.	35.6	37.1	44.7	43.3	42.4
Total	200.0	200.0	200.0	200.0	200.0	200.0	200.0	200.0	200.0

Notes: Data for April 1989 exclude domestic trading involving the Deutsche mark in Germany.

Sources: BIS, Triennial Central Bank Survey of Foreign Exchange and Derivatives Market Activity (available at http://www.bis.org/publ/rpfx13.htm?m=6%7C35).

amount of RMB used for trade settlement amounted to USD1.7 trillion at the end of 2013.

Despite these early successes, it is true that the RMB has its own challenges to overcome. In terms of daily turnover (see Table 3), the RMB still has a long way to go before becoming a significant player. Moreover, China's capital account is relatively closed (Lee *et al.* 2013), and the RMB does not have enough market liquidity to cater for large volumes of transactions of financial flows. Yet, despite the embryonic state of the RMB, there is no alternative to the USD. The euro will not likely increase its influence in the global currency market in the foreseeable future either, given the existing economic challenges in Europe.

While the market will ultimately decide which currency it will use, one should not undermine the important role governments play in creating and shaping the framework of the market. With this in mind, if governments coordinate to put in place the rule to the best interest of all parties concerned, the market will respond. While history testifies that global coordination for a change in the IMS is hardly possible, as eloquently argued by Eichengreen (2010), progress was made at the regional level, e.g., the euro, if not at the global level since the Bretton Woods system. This suggests that changes are possible at the regional level, especially if it coincides with the direction the market has already taken.

To address the global imbalance as well as to ride on the growing use of the RMB, Asian economies could agree on an arrangement that will enhance the use of a few key Asian currencies for trade (and services) settlements within the region. As argued by Lee and Park (2014), such an approach would not require opening the capital account prematurely nor waiting until the Asian bond market deepens sufficiently. Instead, it will help to deepen the Asian bond market, and also promote the use of the RMB among Asian economies and beyond before capital account convertibility is attained.

3.2. Possible Framework of a New IMS

The system should be developed first to facilitate the use of local currencies for "settlement" of trade and services, and then gradually expanded to include financial flows. A regional payment system could start with the RMB, the Japanese yen, and a few other Asian currencies including the Korean won, the Singapore dollar, and then perhaps one or all of the large ASEAN counties' currencies, i.e., the Malaysian ringgit, the Thai baht, the Indonesian rupiah and the Philippine peso. At the initial stage, bilateral arrangements between the RMB and respective currencies can be set up, followed by gradual buildup of agreements among the other currencies. Other ASEAN countries whose currencies are not included in the original group of currencies can still join by agreeing to use any of the currencies in the group for their trade settlement. Once the framework is set up, it would consist of ASEAN+3 countries and perhaps four to five currencies.

The RMB internationalization steps already taken can provide some guide on how to proceed. In this regard, China–Japan financial cooperation would be somewhat irrelevant as it is an agreement between a convertible currency and a semi-convertible currency. The setting up of RMB centers in London, Paris, Luxembourg, Australia, and Canada would also fall under this category as they are markets for RMB and convertible currency transactions. The bilateral arrangements between China's mainland and Taiwan, or China and Singapore, however, would be more relevant for others to follow as the currencies traded against the RMB are both non-convertible. Since both involve the use of RMB and not so much the reciprocal use of the other currencies, more proactive policies may be called for promoting the use of the other currencies as well. So far, China–South Korea's agreement is completely one-sided, allowing only the RMB to be used for trade and services settlements.

RMB internationalization started in Hong Kong SAR (Special Administrative Region). It is a part of China and hence may not be fully applicable to other countries. Yet, the institutional framework which is already in place is most advanced, thanks to the extensive cooperation between the PBC and the Hong Kong Monetary Authority (HKMA) and a large share of offshore RMB transactions in Hong Kong. Thus, Hong Kong provides useful lessons for others.

a. Lessons from Hong Kong SAR

The beginning can be traced back to 2003 with China approving the introduction of personal RMB business in Hong Kong. Since the implementation of this policy in 2005, RMB deposits in local banks have grown on the back of demand from individuals as well as businesses. The introduction of the trade settlement pilot system in mid-2009 and the subsequent extension to 20 provinces and to trading partners from all countries in 2010, the partial opening of China's interbank bond market to eligible offshore investors in 2010, and the launch of offshore RMB product in 2011 all contributed to the rapid pickup in RMB deposits in 2011 from around RMB60 billion at the beginning of 2010 to about RMB700 billion at the end of 2011.

While implementation may be complex, the underlying concept is simple enough. It is essentially supplying RMB through trade, providing a platform to hold the RMB in Hong Kong by offering RMB products locally as well as opening a partial window for investment in the mainland capital market, and then promoting the use of the RMB. The latter includes offering relatively attractive returns. One factor that contributed to the rapid growth in demand for the RMB was the fact that Hong Kong is part of China; the RMB was a convenient way for increasing cross-border trade with the mainland; and most of all, there was a strong expectation of RMB appreciation. For local banks, they were willing to make short-term losses by paying a small premium on RMB deposits in order to position themselves better for the expected growth of RMB business in Hong Kong and worldwide.

Practical steps started with nominating a clearing bank[3] and establishing a payment system, including the delivery of RMB cash notes. With the growth of RMB business, Hong Kong has established a comprehensive and sophisticated multi-currency platform for clearing and settling financial transactions. The Central Money Market Unit (CMU), the computerized clearing and settlement facilities for Hong Kong dollars (HKD) and foreign currency bonds, is now linked with the Real Time Gross Settlement System (RTGS) for interbank payments in HKD, USD, euro, and RMB to ensure, *inter alia*, the delivery and payment of debt instruments at the end of the transaction day. Moreover, the CMU is now also linked to the China

---

[3]Clearing banks: China Construction Bank: London; Bank of China: Frankfurt, Hong Kong, Taipei, Paris, Australia; ICBC: Singapore, Luxemburg, Canada; Bank of Communications: Seoul.

Central Depository Trust and Clearing Co., and those in Australia, New Zealand, South Korea, as well as Euroclear and Clearstream.

The RMB RTGS in Hong Kong allows banks outside greater China to settle their RMB transactions with correspondent banks in Hong Kong. This provides a unique advantage for Hong Kong as an RMB offshore center that is made possible through close collaboration between PBC and HKMA and Hong Kong's robust financial infrastructure. As other financial centers catch up with the RMB offshore business, Hong Kong is firmly maintaining its lead and enjoys first-mover advantages as well as its unique relations with the mainland. It has by far the largest offshore liquidity, handling about 80 percent of the total RMB cross-border trade settlement business, 80 percent of global RMB payments, and offers a platform for primary bond issuance and secondary market for RMB products. While RMB business is also picking up in Singapore and London, the magnitude is still small.

The China International Payment System (CIPS) will likely be launched later in 2015, which will greatly reduce the cost as well as time of RMB transactions. This will then bypass one of the offshore centers with RMB clearing banks such as Hong Kong, Singapore, London or a corresponding bank in China's mainland. The latest SWIFT data[4] from June 2015 shows that 1,081 financial institutions already use the RMB for payments with China and Hong Kong, which represents 35 percent of all institutions. In the Asia-Pacific, 37 percent of all financial institutions use the RMB, followed by Europe with 33 percent. In terms of value, the RMB accounts for 2.18 percent of all currencies used for cross-border payments.

To the extent that China's capital account is only partially open, China has to compensate for the lack of access to the financial market in the mainland. Main RMB products are bank deposits/certificates, dim sum bonds, inward FDI in RMB, and RMB qualified Foreign Institutional Investors (RQFII). The RQFII was launched in Hong Kong in 2011, which was then expanded to Singapore, the UK, and France. As of 2014, RQFII

---

[4] Swift RMB Monthly Tracker 2015, available at: http://www.swift.com/assets/swift_com/documents/products_services/RMB_June_2015_final.pdf.

quota distribution to these regions was RMB270 billion (Hong Kong), RMB80 billion (UK), RMB50 billion (Singapore), and RMB80 billion (France). Eligible fund companies, securities firms, and banks can invest in interbank bond market and securities market using their RMB through the RQFII scheme. This partial access to the mainland interbank market has provided a useful platform for holding RMB in offshore centers as well as a clear signal of the direction China is taking toward full liberalization of the capital account (Deutsche Bank AG, 2014).

b. With or Without Currency Swaps

China has signed currency swap agreements with 32 countries and districts as of May 2015 worth RMB3.1 trillion, partly to support RMB internationalization. It has served its purpose well to the extent that an increasingly number of countries are settling trade transactions in RMB. However, the proposal to use some Asian currencies for settlement of current account transactions within the region can be facilitated with or without the use of currency swaps.

In the case a currency swap is used (Figure 5), central banks in both countries play the part of intermediation. For example, at the request of

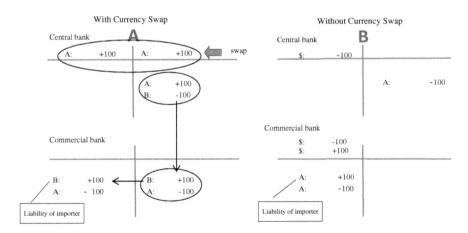

Figure 5. Implication on the Balance Sheet

Sources: This illustration is based on Bank of Korea (2012).

the importer (via a designated bank), the central bank in the importing country transmits a request to its counterpart in the exporting country to pay the equivalent amount in the swapped currency to the exporter (again, via an agent of the designated bank). The trade is then settled between the designated bank in the importing country and the agent of the designated bank in the exporting country. In this process, the swap line has been activated between the two central banks. Unless a similar reversed request is made for transaction settlement, the swap will have to be rolled over. Until then, the ultimate liability of the used amount rests with the central bank of the importer.

Settling trade does not need *ex ante* a local currency swap as long as an agreement is reached between two central banks to allow the use of each other's currencies for that purpose. In addition to the need for designating banks and agents as in the previous case, the central bank of the importing country has to provide financial instruments denominated in its own currency to the exporting country.

c. Extending Bilateral Payments Agreement

Bilateral agreements among ASEAN+3 will require modified versions of the mainland and Hong Kong framework. The financial arrangement is already more advanced than perceived as China has RMB settlement schemes with ASEAN countries, South Korea, Taiwan, and Japan. It also has various RMB instruments available that these countries can tap. Yet, in most cases, trade settlements are one-sided and need to be expanded to include both sides of the flow. Bilateral agreements are required among ASEAN countries, Taiwan, and South Korea, and all countries need to agree on the use of a mutually determined set of currencies for trade settlements. The procedures and institutional framework would be identical to that of the mainland and Hong Kong.

In the case of South Korea, for example, it will have to first set up a won trading center in China (reciprocal to the RMB market in Seoul) to ensure that trade settlement takes place both ways. At the same time, a won offshore center in Singapore could be considered as it has a deep financial market as well as the necessary infrastructure such as the Continuous Linked Settlement System, already with most of the major currencies being traded to ensure minimum exposure to foreign exchange settlement risks. It also has a benefit of being the hub for Chinese companies to reach ASEAN countries. South Korea's trade settlements can then take place in Shanghai and Seoul for bilateral trade flows between South Korea and China, and in Singapore for trade flows between South Korea and ASEAN countries. A won offshore center in Tokyo would serve trade flows between South Korea and Japan, completing the network for South Korea. Other ASEAN countries can follow similar steps to make the network complete.

d. Possible Evolution Including an Asian Version of SDR (Special Drawing Rights)

The financial arrangement among ASEAN+3 has such an advantage that these countries can use their own currencies for trade settlements and invest in each other's territories using respective currencies. For the global economy, it will benefit from Asian currencies moving closer to each other as respective authorities will have stronger incentive to reduce volatility among Asian currencies. This will eventually mean more independent movements of Asian currencies from the USD or the euro, offering the US a greater degree of monetary policy independence.

As such, a benchmark index could be devised that authorities from ASEAN+3 countries could track as a guide for their smooth operations. The use of such a benchmark, which for the sake of convenience can be called ABC (Asian Benchmark Currency), can be expanded later as a unit of account for Chiang Mai Initiative Multilateralization (CMIM) reserve assets as well as other strengthened versions of foreign exchange safety nets (a topic that goes beyond the scope of this chapter). Bonds can be denominated in the ABC, rather than in respective currencies, which will provide a natural hedge for investors in the region. Figure 6 shows one possible compilation of the ABC that uses GDP based on purchasing power parity as the share of the RMB, the yen, the won, the Singapore dollar, and the Malaysian ringgit as relative weights. A closer alignment of individual currencies with this benchmark would reduce volatility and allow for greater monetary independence from the USD.

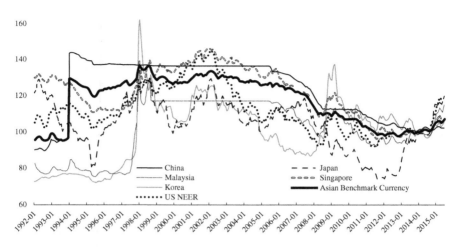

Figure 6.   Asian Benchmark Currency 2013 (M1 = 100)

4. Incentives and Risks for Member Countries

The benefits of such a system are many. First of all, it will allow countries involved to reduce the share of the USD in their reserves to the extent that they will be able to finance their intra-Asia trade with their own currencies. As countries start using their currencies directly for settlements, policy efforts will be directed toward reducing the volatility between bilateral exchange rates that hitherto have been determined as cross exchange rates. Greater stability among Asian currencies in turn promotes intra-Asia trade and a greater use of the global value chain within Asia. Finally, it will also benefit the United States as these currencies collectively will become more flexible *vis-à-vis* the USD, breaking the reverse spillover of its own monetary policy. The corollary is that this will also dampen monetary policy transmission from the US to the EMs.

The USD, the euro, and the RMB will be the main trading currencies, with the British sterling, and the Japanese yen each playing a relatively minor role at the global level. Other smaller currencies will play their part at the regional level, but it is doubtful whether the market would use them significantly beyond their respective geographical region. Rather, smaller currencies will likely gravitate around one of these three major currencies.

While a single world currency, or at least a global unit of account such as the SDR, would be a more efficient system, it is hardly feasible. Even if such an agreement were to be concluded, active promotion by governments would be required to move the market to use such a world currency — likely to no avail. The tri-polar currency cluster system, on the other hand, will be something that the market will shape by itself with only a limited support from governments once a currency arrangement is set up in Asia.

4.1. Incentives

The benefits of such a financial arrangement for individual countries are as follows. For China, it will hasten the RMB internationalization process in Asia beyond Hong Kong. The RMB business will likely pick up quickly, especially given the extensive Global Value Chains (GVCs) among ASEAN+3 countries, without the need to open up its capital account. To the extent that rapid capital account convertibility will pose risks in domestic financial markets, internalization of the RMB within the region as a first step without raising the stake would be good news for China.

For Japan, the benefit will likely be smaller as its currency is already fully convertible. However, it will promote the use of the yen in Asian countries for trade settlements beyond trade flows with Japan or for yen carry trade. A more important benefit would be the reduced exposure to foreign exchange risks of its debt financing. Since the appetite for further debt instrument by its residents appear to be waning, selling yen-denominated assets will reduce Japan's foreign exchange exposure to non-resident investors.

For South Korea, the benefit is yet again different from the above two cases and will mostly come from the reduced need to hold a large amount of foreign exchange reserves in convertible currencies, especially the euro and the USD. In addition, a more diverse combination of currencies, according to trade shares and investment positions with other ASEAN+3 countries, will help reduce valuation losses. For example, South Korea's trade is skewed toward raw material and capital goods, especially with China, reflecting the growing linkages through the global value chain (see Table 4). The benefits to ASEAN countries will be similar to South Korea,

Table 4. Korea: Direction of Trade with top 10 Trading Partners by Type, 2013–2014 (In Percentage of Total)

	Raw Material	Capital Goods	Consumer Goods	Total	Raw Materials	Capital Goods	Consumer Goods	Total
China	8.0	11.5	5.1	24.6	11.5	21.8	1.9	35.2
Japan	8.4	7.0	0.8	16.2	4.4	2.5	1.2	8.1
Singapore	1.1	2.0	0.0	3.1	2.6	2.8	0.1	5.6
Taiwan	0.7	3.4	0.2	4.3	1.9	1.6	0.2	3.7
Vietnam	0.6	0.4	1.2	2.2	2.1	2.8	0.4	5.3
Hong Kong	0.1	0.3	0.1	0.5	1.6	4.6	0.4	6.7
Indonesia	3.1	0.1	0.4	3.6	2.0	0.5	0.2	2.8
USA	4.5	5.5	2.3	12.3	3.8	7.0	5.1	16.0
EU	6.0	7.7	3.2	16.8	3.3	6.3	2.6	12.2
Saudi Arabia	10.6	0.0	0.0	10.6	0.5	0.8	0.8	2.1
	48	38	14	100	35	51	14	100

Sources: K-Stat; KITA database and author's calculation.

although some of the less advanced countries may find it difficult to handle multiple currencies in their cross-border settlements. These countries could start with one or two currencies and then expand later as their financial infrastructure develops.

4.2. Risks

The risks are again different in each of the countries involved. There is no apparent risk to Japan as its exchange rate is already fully flexible. The impact of its quantitative easing (QE) policy on the yen exchange rate might be reduced, although it is not clear whether this is good or bad for the Japanese economy as it has already exceeded 120 yen/USD, taxing consumer welfare. For China, the key risk is loss of control over its exchange rate. Yet, to the extent that it still has a firm grip on its capital flows, and the scale of the economy is very large relative to capital flows, the risk appears to be minimal.

For South Korea and Singapore, the risk is probably highest as both have fully convertible capital account and flexible exchange rate. For South Korea, in particular, with a higher concentration in manufacturing industries and a relatively less deep financial market, loss of control over the won exchange rate could pose stability risks. The situation has improved somewhat from the early 2000s when South Korea was exposed to volatile offshore Non-Deliverable Forward (NDF) market with spillover onto the onshore won spot market. However, the scope of NDF playing a destabilizing role will soon wane once the market realizes that the central bank will not intervene and they will be paying against themselves, rather than betting on some policy response from the monetary authorities. As shown in Table 5, the growth of the RMB liquidity tends to reduce the NDF share of the trading — a trend also seen in Hong Kong China Offshore Spot in foreign exchange market.

Moreover, South Korea and other Asian economies have raised the stock of international reserves during the mid-2000s to an adequate level that would discourage a speculative attack on the currency, be it on- or offshore (Figure 7), unless its value is clearly perceived to be off than what would be consistent with market fundamentals. Lastly, South Korea has rarely intervened in the foreign exchange market other than to contain

Table 5.　Summary of London Trading Forex Products (Average Daily Value in US $Million)

	2011 FY	2012 H1	2012 FY	2013 H1	2013 FY	2014 H1
Deliverable						
Spot & forward	1444	2842	3784	7461	7899	21047
Swaps & options	1086	2686	3942	8096	10768	21370
Total deliverable	**2,530**	**5,528**	**7,726**	**15,557**	**18,667**	**42,417**
Non-deliverable						
Forwards	4,945	3,722	4,889	3,679	3,493	5,565
Swaps & options	3,149	2,379	4,234	3,081	3,125	6,670
Total non-deliverable	**8,094**	**6,101**	**9,123**	**6,760**	**6,618**	**12,235**
Total	**10,624**	**11,629**	**16,849**	**22,317**	**25,285**	**54,625**

Sources: Bourse Consult and City of London (2014).

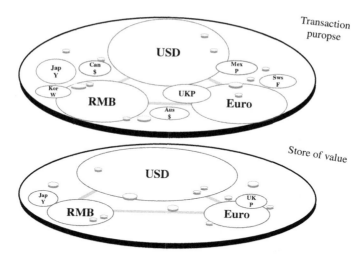

Figure 7. The Tri-Polar and Two-Tier System

excess volatility since the global financial crisis. Indeed, the error terms of the won regression exercise with and without reserves changes show[5] that intervention was relatively frequent and large in scope before the global financial crisis (Figure 8), but rare since then. These developments argue that the risk of a speculative attack in one of the offshore NDF market would not have any notable impact on onshore spot market. Moreover, macroprudential measures would serve as useful tools to ensure a smooth transition into full won convertibility.

Other ASEAN countries would need to be careful to liberalize their capital account or provide an alternative source of investment instruments in their respective currencies without exposing their positions to a possible speculative attack. In this regard, only selective ASEAN countries should offer their currencies as a part of the settlement currencies at the

---

[5] Derived from a panel regression on the exchange rate including the reserve change as one of its exogenous variables. With reserves changes are the error terms of the regression and without reserve changes are what the errors would have been under zero change in reserves. The difference then is a measure of how much the exchange rate moved due to reserve changes (a proxy for intervention).

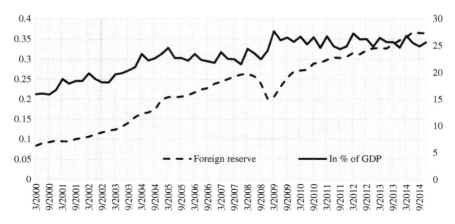

Figure 8.   Korea: Foreign Reserves (In Trillion USD)

Sources: World Economic Outlook, IMF, and CEIC (2014).

beginning, and gradually join the group while taking part in using other local currencies for their trade settlement.

4.3. Other Economic Considerations

A challenge still remains to ensure that the market responds to the joint effort of promoting internationalization of the local currencies (other than the RMB and the yen) in Asia, placing the institutional structure, including settlement and clearing system, the efficiency of the direct interbank market for local currencies, and the adequacy of instruments, to hold these currencies in the region. At the other extreme, there is also a concern that the demand for these local currencies may expand beyond the region, especially during times of greater exchange rate volatility. While the market liquidity of the RMB and the yen are deep enough to cater for large-scale and sudden shifts in demand, speculative attacks in other local currencies may not be able to absorb such shocks except through large variations in their value.

RMB internationalization was accompanied by supplying cash notes to Hong Kong. While such an arrangement may be difficult for all participating countries, it could be applied to countries with common border after local currency usage on both borders takes off. For example, South Korea and China could use each other's currencies in the northeast part of China, and Malaysia and Singapore could also use each other's currencies.

Additional benefit could be obtained by utilizing this currency arrangement for expanding the regional financial safety net. To start with, the currency arrangement by itself will strengthen the regional safety net as exposure among the member countries can now be addressed through the use of local currencies, rather than in any of the reserve currencies. Moreover, the CMIM commitments by member countries could be partially in one of the local currencies used in addition to reserve currencies, the limits of which could be determined by the net exposure of the region to the rest of the world. In other words, of the USD240 billion currently committed under the CMIM, a third could be in local currencies, especially in RMB, to the extent a shock in the foreign exchange market in member countries may be due to exposures that originated from liabilities among themselves. Alternatively, any additional increase in the commitment can be done in Asia's local currencies.

4.4. Geopolitical Challenges

A currency arrangement will help economic integration among Asian economies, which in turn will contribute to instituting geopolitical stability in Northeast Asia. On the other hand, if the current geopolitical tension in the region deteriorates, it could impede progress in shaping such a currency arrangement. Thus, economic benefits from the currency arrangement and more generally from economic integration will need to be clearly explained to the general public to have a positive impact in shaping security and political decisions. For example, China's "Belt and Road Initiative" can benefit from such a currency arrangement as those countries directly affected by the initiative will not have to resort to hard currencies for investment and trade with China and also between each other. Given that most emerging and developing economies' activities are constrained by the availability of hard currency, this will allow for greater freedom in implementing the initiative.

At the same time, it will also benefit the US and other countries that will become members of the Trans-Pacific Partnership (TPP). The US has expressed concerns about exchange rate market interventions in some Asian economies and has indicated that the TPP could have provisions that will allow the US to respond with trade measures against such behavior. Since the proposed currency arrangement in Asia will lead to smaller cross exchange rate volatility among members' currencies but greater swings, on average against the US dollar, it will also reduce the chance of the US ever having to invoke that provision.

5. Conclusion

The current IMS is a market outcome of the institutional arrangement that was put in place by key global players, including those at the Bretton Woods conference, as well as the complex and dynamic process of globalization. Initially starting with the gold standard, global sentiment moved from favoring the fixed exchange regime to favoring greater flexibility. A global unit of account, the SDR, was introduced but was not taken up by the market partly due to the lack of a framework that would define its uses beyond the scope of the Bretton Woods institutions. Regional currency arrangements, regional single currency, and exchange bands were tested with limited success.

It is not clear whether there is necessarily an *ex ante* optimal system with respect to the number of reserve currencies, regional or global currency arrangements, and the type of exchange rate regime. Yet, the system proposed in this chapter provides an alternative to the current IMS that will be able to address some of the existing shortcomings. The proposed arrangement, if successfully implemented by the authorities concerned, will facilitate payments for "settlement" of trade and services in local currencies with the specified Asian economies. This will naturally involve financial flows as holders of local currencies will try to optimize the returns as well as the value over time by diversifying in currencies and instruments.

As a store of value, it will take some time before the non-USD currencies in the tri-polar cluster can catch up to even partly replace the currently US dollar-dominated assets. This is fine since even during the transition period, this hybrid system will be able to overcome current shortcomings, including global imbalance, without unduly disrupting the current order.

References

Bank of Korea (2012). Press Release: Introduction of Korea–China Currency

Bourse Consult and City of London (2014). London RMB business volumes January–June 2014: City of London renminbi series. Policy Practitioner Paper. London: City of London Corporation.

CEIC (2014). Foreign Reserves in the Republic of Korea, March 2000 to September 2014. Available from CEIC database.

Chen, Hongyin, Wenshen Peng and Chang Shu (2009). The Potential of the Renminbi as an International Currency. Working Paper No. 182009. Hong Kong: Hong Kong Institute for Monetary Research.

Choi, Woon Gyu and Il Houng Lee (2010). Monetary Transmission of Global Imbalances in Asian Countries. Working Paper 10/214. Washington, DC: International Monetary Fund.

Deutsche Bank AG (2014). At the center of RMB internationalization: A brief guide to offshore RMB.

Eichengreen, Barry (1998). The Euro as a Reserve Currency. *Journal of the Japanese and International Economies*, 12(4): 483–503.

Eichengreen, Barry (2010). Managing a Multiple Reserve Currency World. *Insights*, 8(Nov 2010): 29–33.

Huo, Wei-dong, Jia Wang and Xing Shu (2014). Has the Renminbi the potential to become an international reserve currency? Paper submitted to the international conference of "Korea and the World Economy XIII: 'New Challenges for Trans-regionalism in the Asia-Pacific,'" Association of Korean Economic Studies, Seoul, June 2014.

Kenen, Peter (1983). The Role of the Dollar as an International Reserve Currency. *Occasional Papers* No 13. Group of Thirty. Washington, DC: International Monetary Fund.

Lee, Il Houng (2012). The Current International Monetary System and Future Prospects. Seminar at Jilin University, Chang Chun, China, August 2.

Lee, Il Houng (2013). RMB Internationalization and the Currency Arrangement. Seminar at Asia Economic Forum, Beijing, China, October 28–29.

Lee, Il Houng (2015). Global Imbalance: A Policy Mishap or a Rational Outcome? The Case of Korea. *World Economy Update*, 5(8): 1–7.

Lee, Il Houng and Da Young Yang (2014). Is More Investment the Answer to Deficient Global Demand? *World Economy Update*, 4(14): 1–3.

Lee, Il Houng and Yung Chul Park (2014). Use of National Currencies for Trade Settlement in East Asia: A Proposal. ADBI Working Paper No. 474. Tokyo: Asian Development Bank Institute.

Lee, Il Houng, Xu Qingjun, and Murtaza Syed (2013). China's Demography and Its Implications. IMF Working Paper 13/82. Washington, DC: International Monetary Fund.

Lee, Il Houng, Murtaza Syed, and Liu Xueyan (2013). China's Path to Consumer-based Growth: How to Identify and Reduce Excessive Investment. IMF Working Paper, WP/13/83. Washington, DC: International Monetary Fund.

Menzie, Chinn and Jeffrey Frankel (2005). Will the Euro Eventually Surpass the Dollar as Leading International Reserve Currency? NBER Working Paper No. 11510. Cambridge, Massachusetts: National Bureau of Economic Research.

Mundell, Robert A. (1997). The International Monetary System in the 21st Century: Could Gold Make a Comeback? Lecture delivered at St. Vincent College, Letrobe, Pennsylvania, March 12.

People's Bank of China Study Group (2006). The Timing, Path, and Strategies of RMB Internationalization. *China Finance*, 5, 12–13.

Swap-Financed Trade Settlement Facility. Available at http://www.bok.or.kr/down.search?file_path=/attach/eng/634/2012/12/1354590679949.pdf&file_name=20121204_press+release_%28engl%29.pdf (accessed October 15, 2015).

Wu, Jun, Yingli Pan and Qi Zhu (2014). The conditions and potential of RMB as an international reserve currency: The empirical evidences from the history of eight major international reserve currencies. *China Finance Review International*, 4(2): 103–123.

Chapter 6

Conclusion

Yung Chul Park and Il Houng Lee

Despite the huge literature on the structural weaknesses and the numerous proposals for the reform of the international monetary system (IMS), it seems that few initiatives are appealing and agreeable to both advanced and emerging economies. Since 2011, G20 members have lost much of their interest in the reform of the IMS simply because not only they cannot agree on what they should and could do, but also they have been preoccupied with other pressing issues such as recession and deflation.

The future of the international monetary system will greatly depend on the prospects for recovery in the euro zone and the rise of China. If the euro-zone economies improve from the ongoing crisis and succeed in reforming the weaknesses of the euro architecture and China continues to expand along its current soft landing path, the pressure for reform will grow. However, such pressure alone does not necessarily lead to the creation of a new system but requires governments to provide the basic framework analogous to developments in a certain locality requiring basic physical infrastructure. Agreements among governments in Asia to use their respective currencies for the settlement of current account transactions could promote the RMB to become a more globally used currency without China fully opening its capital account. In this process, the use of other participating currencies will expand beyond their own borders, but largely be limited to the Asia region. In due course, the world's currency arrangement will become a three-pillar system consisting of the US dollar, the Chinese RMB, and the euro. This will contribute to reducing the global imbalance as Asia's currencies will start moving closer to each other, making monetary policy in the US more independent.

On the other hand, if the euro-zone crisis drags on and Chinese authorities face difficulty in engineering a soft landing, an unlikely scenario for now, then the state of confusion and uncertainty of the global economy will muddle through without knowing where it is heading. It would take a major global crisis for G20 leaders to attempt to restart the reform of the international monetary system.

Index

ASEAN, 13, 16, 17, 20–22, 30, 31, 57, 63, 64, 66

ASEAN+3, 9–11, 13–15, 17, 21, 30, 31, 40, 45, 63–66, 73, 134, 142, 146, 147, 149

ASEAN+3 Macroeconomic Regional Office (AMRO), 63

ASEAN-5, 11–13, 15, 17, 20, 31, 41, 45

ASEAN Economic Community, 31

ASEAN Summit, 31

Asian Bond Markets Development Initiative (ABMI), 64

Asian currencies, 131, 134, 141, 142, 145, 147, 148

Asian Development Bank, 14, 25

Asian economies, 134, 141, 151, 155, 156

Asian financial crisis, 9, 14, 63, 66, 132

Australian dollar, 25

Bank of Canada (BOC), 70

Bank of England (BOE), 70

Bank of Japan (BOJ), 70

Bank of Korea, 26, 32

Bretton Woods, 50, 141, 156

BRICs (Brazil, Russia, India, China), 72, 73

British sterling, 136, 148

capital account, 141, 144, 145, 149, 151, 153

capital flows, 151

Chiang Mai Initiative (CMI), 63

Chiang Mai Initiative Multilateralization (CMIM), 9, 51, 147, 155

China, 9–22, 24–26, 28–32, 39, 41–45, 56, 57, 59, 63–66, 70, 72, 73, 133, 134, 136–139, 142–147, 149, 151, 155

clearing systems, 154

CMIM Precautionary Line (CMIM-PL), 64

CMIM Stability Facility (CMIM-SF), 64

Credit Default Swap (CDS), 72

Cross-border trade settelement, 23, 29, 56

cross-border trade transactions, 22

cross-border transactions, 131

currency arrangement
  regional currency arrangement, 30, 156

currency convertibility, 41

currency internationalization, 11, 20, 31, 42, 45

currency scheme, 11, 12, 14, 20, 21, 30, 37, 39–43, 45

currency settlement scheme, 31

currency swap agreement, 26
current account
  balance, 132
  deficit, 86, 88, 90, 96, 132, 133
  surplus, 132, 133

Dim Sum bond, 25

EC (European Community), 77, 87,
  111–114
economic mismanagement, 6
Economic Review and Policy
  Dialogue (ERPD), 63
emergency liquidity assistance
  (ELA), 91
Emerging Markets (EMs), 59, 72, 131
Euro, 10, 13, 15, 25, 39–41
euro-area crisis, 79–81, 89, 94–96,
  105, 110, 115, 116, 118
European Central Bank (ECB), 69
European Economic and Monetary
  Union (EEMU), 77
European Financial Stability Facility
  (EFSF), 101
European Monetary Union, 55
European Stability Mechanism
  (ESM), 67, 91
Euro Working Group (EWG), 112
Ex Post Assessments (EPA), 79
Ex Post Evaluation (EPE), 103
Extended Fund Facility (EEF),
  79, 87

Federal Reserve, 44, 45, 67, 69
financial market, 54, 136, 139, 146, 151
financial reform, 10, 11, 21, 31, 42
fiscal deficit, 88, 93
Flexible Credit Lines (FCL), 69
free trade agreements, 10, 13

free trade area, 56
Free Trade Area of the Asia-Pacific
  (FTAAP), 14

G7, 72
G20, 49, 50, 60, 66, 67, 69, 71–73,
  159, 160
Global Development Horizons
  (GDH), 59
global financial crisis, 5, 9, 13, 14,
  17, 21, 44, 49, 52, 62, 64, 67, 131,
  139, 153
global imbalances, 132
global safety net, 67, 68
Global Value Chains (GVCs), 149
Greek crisis, 77, 79, 88, 89, 92, 114

High-Access Standby Arrangement
  (HAPA), 69
Hong Kong, 13, 21, 22, 24, 25, 28,
  29, 33, 143–146, 149, 151, 154
Hong Kong Monetary Authority
  (HKMA), 24, 142

Indonesia, 13, 17, 18, 41, 150
interbank market, 24, 25
international currency, 2
internationalization, 134–138, 142,
  145, 149, 154
international monetary system (IMS),
  1, 21, 45, 49, 131
international reserves, 132, 138, 151
intra-industry trade, 12, 17, 19, 21
intra-regional trade, 10, 12, 14–16, 20

Japan, 9, 11–21, 28, 30–32, 39–43,
  45, 63–66, 70–72, 138, 142, 146,
  147, 149, 151
Japanese yen, 134, 136, 138, 142, 148

Korea, 9, 11–21, 26, 30–33, 38–41, 43–45, 57, 62–65, 67, 70, 72
Korean won, 39, 40

Lehman Brothers, 51, 69
liquidity support system, 63, 65, 66

Malaysia, 18, 27, 28, 34, 35, 41, 155
Malaysian ringgit, 24, 58, 142, 147
monetary policy independence, 147

National Asset Management Agency (NAMA), 104
Nonperforming Loans (NPLs), 128

offshore center, 144, 146, 147

People's Bank of China (PBC), 21, 24, 26, 28, 137, 138
Philippines, 18, 34, 35
policy reform, 31
Precautionary Credit Lines (PCL), 69

Regional Comprehensive Economic Partnership (RCEP), 13
regionalization, 131, 134, 138
reserve currency, 21, 26, 31, 40, 42–44, 50–55, 72, 135–139
RMB, 51–57, 70, 134–139, 141–149, 151, 154, 155
RMB internationalization, 10, 21, 22, 41, 44, 45, 57
RMB settlement, 22, 24

Singapore, 9, 18, 24, 33, 44, 134, 142–147, 151, 155
Singapore dollar, 134, 142, 147
Society for Worldwide Interbank Financial Telecommunication (SWIFT), 56
South Korea, 133, 144, 146, 147, 149, 151, 155
Special Drawing Rights (SDR), 51, 53
Stability and Growth Pact (SCP), 90
Swiss National Bank (SNB), 70, 71

Taiwan, 142, 146, 150
Thailand, 18, 27, 34, 35
Thailand Baht, 142
trade settlements, 10, 11, 32, 33
Trans-Pacific Partnership (TPP), 155
troika program, 92–94

United Kingdom (UK), 139, 144, 145, 153
United States (US), 52, 54, 131–133, 139, 148
unremunerated reserve requirements (URR), 61
US dollar (USD), 10, 21, 25, 30, 32, 37, 39–41, 44, 45, 50–51, 52, 54, 55, 68, 71, 131

Vietnam, 150
VIX, 51